DUMP YOUR DEBT

Using the Tools of Financial Crisis Management
So your income goes *in* the bank and not *to* the bank.

KEN GROSS

Talk Show Host and Leader in the Law

OPT Publishing, Inc.

OPT Publishing, Inc.
Financial Publications Department
30150 Telegraph Road
Suite 444
Bingham Farms, Michigan 48025
Fax (248) 645-8225

To contact Ken Gross, email him at kengross@thavgross.com

ISBN-13: 978-0985816308
ISBN-10: 0985816309

To my wife, Bonnie, my side-kick who has always encouraged me to write and pursue new endeavors and my daughters, Amy and Jenny, the two greatest children a father could ever have.

Contents

Forward

So how did it come to pass that I've written *Dump Your Debt?* Originally, this work was to be titled "Had Enough" – and was derived from the frustration I felt and still feel over the Financial Crisis. My guess is that if you are reading this – you have spoken these words to yourself, "I've 'Had Enough' and can barely stand it anymore." In the last three years, I have watched the fundamental aspects of our traditional American way of life crumble to the brink of destruction. I feel betrayed by Wall Street, the banks, credit card companies and our government. I am frustrated and angry!

So what is the point of *Dump Your Debt?* It is simple and built on four key assumptions:

- Our government is not capable of addressing the needs of people who have been victimized by the loss in property values and income by the Financial Crisis.

- The adversity caused by the Great Recession has correspondingly created great opportunity to shed debt and preserve future income if you are able to properly identify the opportunity and take action.

- We are all victims of the Financial Crisis. Even if you have been fortunate not to lose your job or income – your property values and net worth have been depleted through no fault of your own – *and you owe it to yourself to do whatever you can do to recapture or minimize your loss.*

- You will be sad (and possibly broke) if you pass up the opportunity now to get rid of your debt and begin to start saving your future income.

By way of background, I'm a business attorney who has practiced law in Metropolitan Detroit for 30 years. My specialty has always been assisting the small to mid-size business and their owners through good times and bad times. Today – we are facing bad times. Michigan, with its automotive dependence, has certainly suffered – but the reality is that many, many good people throughout this country are suffering. In November, 2008 – when the automobile industry, financial and real estate markets all came tumbling down – I reacted by starting *The Financial Crisis Talk Center* radio show which airs Saturday mornings in the Metropolitan Detroit market and developing the discipline I have named, "Financial Crisis Management."

The essence of Financial Crisis Management is that before you determine which strategy or combination of strategies is right for you – i.e., short sale, loan modification, bankruptcy, debt resolution or settlement – you need to analyze the potential tax consequences, cost, benefit and risk of the alternatives to determine the proper course. If you seek the advice of someone who only offers one or two of the various services – you will *not* receive objective advice because that person will be biased in their desire to sell you their service. This book and Financial Crisis Management eliminates this issue – because all potential services are evaluated in order to identify the combination that provides the optimal result at the least cost.

Over the last three years – I watched with dismay as the Federal Government wasted hundreds of millions of dollars on foolish and ineffective programs designed to assist the housing and foreclosure problem. We have witnessed the banks ineffectively and callously foreclose on homes in the midst of modification programs that are poorly administered with borrowers being misled as to their legal rights while documents are lost, fraudulently signed and homes foreclosed. On top of that, thousands of flimflam con artists have professed to be experts peddling loan modification, short sale assistance and debt settlement services that sell people services not based on what they need but rather based on the seller's desire to turn a quick buck at the expense of the person's last reserved savings. In many instances, because the tax ramifications of cancelation of debt were not evaluated before the strategy was picked, people have ended up with large income tax liabilities that are nondischargeable in bankruptcy that could have been easily avoided.

As of May, 2012, sixteen million Americans are underwater in their homes and the average price of homes has fallen 35% from 2008. Nearly 40% of homeowners with a mortgage owe 120% more than their home is worth and 15% owe more than double what the home is worth. This is the "American Dream" turned "American Nightmare." The same people that five years ago were living a good life - one with full time employment, home ownership, good credit, 401(k) or IRA savings – now find themselves unemployed, facing foreclosure, credit ruined and savings exhausted.

Dump Your Debt is designed to lay out for you in plain language and simple strategies the benefit of my experience in helping people survive *and prosper* in the face of mortgage lenders, banks and credit card companies that have no compassion for people and who have allowed their unfettered greed for profit bring our country a dangerous step to the eve of destruction

Dump Your Debt is written for those of you who share my frustration. The premise of this book is that if you have *had enough* then you need a straightforward roadmap of what you can successfully do to leverage these bad times to your benefit. You need to know what works, as well as what doesn't and what lame brain ideas and strategies you should avoid. This book is designed to guide you so that you will know the optimal strategy you should employ to shed your debt and preserve your future income. The contents of this book -- are in the words of an industry that I despise – *priceless*.

Dump Your Debt is dedicated to you, the American public who deserve a better deal than the hand that has been dealt.

                                     Ken Gross

Legal Matters

This book is intended to share my views and experiences with the reader in addressing financial issues particularly in view of the circumstances arising during and from the Financial Crisis. This book is not a substitute for seeking the services of a licensed attorney who is practicing law in the state in which you reside. Nothing contained in this book shall give rise to the creation of a client relationship and the reader shall not have the right to rely upon the opinions, recommendations or suggestions contained in this piece.

With that said, enjoy *Dump Your Debt!*

1

Four Common Horror Stories of the Financial Crisis

(The stories are illustrative only)

The following stories are fictional but illustrate the circumstances that many people have faced in this financial meltdown. I have selected four scenarios that encompass a great majority of the circumstances people have experienced in this crisis. When you read them – see if you can determine which one fits you or your friends the best.

Rich and Fairway Company – Screwed by the Bank

I am sitting with my client, Rich London, in the office of a local bank with Mr. Wallace from the "Special Assets" Department. Also in the meeting is Bill Meadows, Rich's loan officer and friend for the last ten years. Why are we here? Well, Rich has been my client for 20 years. He runs a successful fabrication business – Fairway Company. In fact, Rich is a great client. He's the kind of client that appreciates good service, is polite, successful and pays his bills on time. As a business attorney, what more could you want? For that matter, if you were his bank, you couldn't ask for more. WRONG!!!

This is why and how we got here. You see Rich is current on his credit line with the bank, all payments have been made timely, he is in loan formula under his borrowing agreement and he has $300,000 available to borrow on his credit line. The bank also holds the mortgage on Rich's office/warehouse for $750,000. Last appraised in 2006, the building was valued at $1.3 million. Sound good? Not to the bank. We're here because, last week (Bill Meadows, Rich's loan officer and friend) called Rich. The call went like this:

BILL: Hey Rich - how's it going? How's the fam?

RICH: Good Bill. We're doing okay here considering these tough times. What's up?

BILL: We'll, uh – this is awkward. I just got out of a meeting with the District Manager and I was told to call you and tell you that while we appreciate all the business we've done and recognize that you're a quality customer – we'd like you to shop for a new lender. The Bank has decided to reduce its real estate lending portfolio and Fairway does not fit with the go forward game.

Silence ensues . . .

RICH: What are you saying Bill? I've been with you for 10 years. We have a perfect history. We're profitable. For Pete sakes – you're my friend.

BILL: I'm saying --- right now I hate my job. I'm saying there is not a damn thing I can do.

RICH: Are you calling my loan?

BILL: Oh no. It's not that bad. We need to meet and we'll review your options. Can you make it next Monday, at 3 PM?

RICH: I'll be there.

Rich and I meet in advance of the meeting. Rich, always upbeat and the optimist is certain he can use logic and his stellar history with the bank to turn things around. I do not share the optimism since this is the fifth meeting like this that I've attended in the last couple of months and, unlike in days past, I realize the banks are not interested in working with their customers once upper management has made its decision.

We meet in the conference room in the business banking center. We walk into the room and the first bad event unfolds. Bill, rises, shakes Rich's hand and mine (Bill knows me since we've met on a number of deals involving Rich over the years) and introduces the two of us to Mr. Wallace. We shake hands and I ask, "Mr. Wallace, why are you here?" Bill intercedes and says, Steve Wallace is from the Bank's Special Assets Group (a/k/a the Interment Division!) and he'll be handling the account from here on out. I think to myself *"out"* is the operative word – and *screwed is* the more appropriate adjective.

We sit down and Mr. Wallace cuts to the chase. "We're sorry about *your situation* Rich, but the 'Bank' expects you to find a new lender in 90 days otherwise the 'Bank' will seek its remedies under the loan documents." Though I had tried to prepare Rich for this exchange – I could feel the burn under his collar. You see Rich is a good guy, he's honest and hardworking. He also likes to compete and win – in competition he's the kind of guy who will on occasion let the club fly on the links following an errant shot (he's my kind a guy!). Rich keeps his cool and hands Mr. Wallace Fairway's recent financial statement, which shows profit, along with a nicely prepared report and projection put together by his CPA on short notice in response to this meeting.

Mr. Wallace glances at the report, flipping a page or two and obviously not reading the report. He then, ever so slightly shaking his head left and right, gently pushes the report slowly over the table back to Rich, "This is not necessary. The Bank has made its decision and will not revisit this."

Watching this pathetic scene unfold, I'd "had enough." Sitting there, I bit my tongue for a second and then – deliberately raised my right hand with an open hand as if I was a street cop and said, "Stop." All eyes turned to me. When I was sure I had everyone's attention,, I looked directly into Mr. Wallace's eyes – allowing the horizontal lines on my forehead to burrow (this burrowing event also happens after a bad shot on the golf course) and said, "Don't use that word." Silence ensued. Wallace, looking confused, said "What word?" Rich and Bill looked curiously at me – and Rich, knowing me, knew I had something to say for whatever it was worth. After allowing extended silence, I said calmly (in my Clint Eastwood tone), "You're not a Bank!" "Please do not use that word. Banks are in the business of loaning money to businesses. You are not in that business. You used to be in that business. Call yourself an institution, company, organization – I don't care, but do not call yourself a Bank."

So what can Rich do in this situation?

Jeff and Wendy's World Has Changed

Jeff and Wendy Hirsch were living a typical upper middle class family life - living in a nice, 4 bedroom, 3,500 square foot home in the suburbs. Their combined income is $300,000 annually. They have two children – Brent is 18 and Sara is 22. They spend money – and they along with many families like them fueled the robust economy of the last 10 years. When the children were young, they went to summer camp, attended dance class, took piano lessons, tennis lessons and golf lessons and traveled with the soccer and hockey teams. They have a family membership at the local health club and all of them are in good shape, leading active lives. Jeff and Wendy enjoy life and take one to two nice vacations per year – often cruising on Royal Caribbean or Carnival Cruise lines.

Jeff and Wendy always pay their bills on time. Never do they miss a payment. Jeff is well organized – pays the bills online and is protective of maintaining his and Wendy's credit rating.

They put one of their children through college without student loans incurring the tuition, room and board, apartment and transportation expenses that come down the pipe. As a family, they value education and want the best for their children. Costs were secondary. From time to time, when immediate costs exceeded income – they charged the expense. Never were the charges anything excessive in one instance – just as a matter of course. Credit? Well they had 750+ credit scores and plenty of credit. The two of them combined had several cards from Bank of America – since over the last 10 years it seemed that Bank of America had gobbled up all of the other banks and credit card issuers (FleetBoston, Primerica, MBNA, LaSalle Bank, and Countrywide Financial). They also had Amazon Express Gold, Optimal and Glamorwood cards, along with Discover, Capital One and all of the department store cards.

All told, as of the end of 2006, the total they owed in credit card debt was $110,000 – and the total still available on the cards was $120,000. Their home was purchased 10 years earlier. After refinancing a couple of times to pull money out to pay down credit balances and to finance Sara's college costs, they had a first mortgage of $350,000 and a second mortgage of $75,000. The fair market value of the home, at the end of 2006, was $535,000, and their combined 401(k) and IRA accounts were at $100,000.

Back to Jeff and Wendy - it's Saturday night and they are out to dinner with three other couples at a nice supper club. The bill comes – and each couple antes up a credit card instructing the waiter to add 20% to the bill and divide the bill four ways. Jeff uses his Glamourwood card which has a present balance of $9,000, but a credit line of $22,000. He's using this card because he wants to accumulate points which will enable him to obtain a discount on his hotel rate for a vacation that is two months out.

Do you know where this is going?

Five minutes later the waiter returns and informs the table, "Mr. Hirsch you have a telephone call. You can take it at the maître d's stand." Jeff excuses himself and goes to the maître d's stand. The maître d, in a quiet and professional manner, explains to Jeff that his card was declined. Jeff is shocked, indicating that it is not possible. The maître d, apologizing, explains that he even called the credit card company's express merchant service center to make sure there was no computer glitch.

With friends waiting, Jeff is in shock, telling the maître d, "This must be a mistake." Jeff pays his share in cash and the maître d suggests that Jeff use the restroom and he'll have the waiter cash everyone else out and explain that you were at the desk and already signed the tab. Jeff, appreciating the maître d's professionalism thanks him for the effort - all the while burning to call Amazon Express to find out what the hell happened.

Once Jeff and Wendy reach the car, Jeff hands Wendy the keys, asking her to drive because he needs to make a call. Wendy, looking at Jeff, realizes that something is wrong and asks, "What's the matter and who called?" Jeff tells her, "There is something wrong with my Amazon Express and I want to find out what it is right now." Wendy takes the wheel and Jeff pulls out the card, flipping the map light on to read the tiny numbers with the 800 number on the back of his card.

"Your scribble and charge privileges have been suspended." With fist clenched, Jeff asks, "When did this happen?" Responding, the representative says, "We're showing a letter was processed yesterday so I believe you will receive it shortly." Shaking his head and glaring over at Wendy, Jeff ratchets up his voice a notch and states, "I've been a cardholder for 15 years - why didn't you call me and tell me this was happening? Instead, you set me up to be embarrassed. Frankly, I cannot believe this is how you treat your customers. If I did that to my customers, I would be out of business." "Mr. Hirsch, I'm very sorry this happened and for what it's worth, I agree you should have been called. Unfortunately, we have limited staff and the number of credit interventions this week has been high. We do value you as a customer and recognize your many years." Shaking his head, Jeff replies, "Right, you really know how to show your appreciation. So can I ask why you did this to me?" "Of course," says the representative. "The file shows you have too many outstanding accounts with high balances." Mortified, Jeff asks, "Who can I talk to in order to reverse this." "If you like, I can connect you with a credit analyst or you could call back tomorrow or at your convenience." Defeated and tired, Jeff says, "Not tonight. Please mark down in your system how upset I am with the way you have treated me – no warning is inexcusable. I'll call back tomorrow."

"I've been a cardholder for 15 years. Why didn't you call me and tell me this was happening. Instead, you set me up to be embarrassed. Frankly, I cannot believe this is how you treat your customers."

As always, the representative closes with, "I'm sorry about what has happened Mr. Hirsch. Thank you for calling Amazon Express, Goodnight."

Jeff explains the call to Wendy as they drive home in silence. The next day, Jeff calls Amazon Express and speaks to a credit analyst. Polite as ever, Jeff gets nowhere – learning only one thing – a lot of people are very angry with Amazon Express and they do not change their mind.

The next day, the letter from Amazon Express arrives explaining the action that Jeff has already learned of without the benefit of advance notice.

Life's everyday events resume and Jeff and Wendy move on from the Amazon Express episode – with the Glamorwood Card now residing in the second drawer of Jeff's desk – since its use – is useless.

Two weeks later, Jeff is pulling up his driveway and as always, he stops to retrieve the mail. In the box, along with the new *Golf Magazine* he sees four white envelopes with a Bank of America logo. These are not statements and there is an "Important Notice" indication of the envelope. Entering the house through the foyer, he opens the first envelope to find a letter addressed to him, listing his account number and informing him that Bank of America, though valuing his business, loyalty and long standing relationship, is reducing his credit line on the account. The reduction is to $100 above his current balance. When Jeff opens envelope 2, 3 and 4, he finds the exact same message for each of the other accounts. "Great, that's just frigging great." Two days later, Jeff's visit to the mailbox yields two more letters – this time from Amazon Express informing of the same action on his Optimal and Amazon Express Gold Accounts. Shaking his head, Jeff realizes that the walls are closing in on him and his available credit is all but evaporated.

The weeks to come do not fare well for Jeff and Wendy. The mailbox (Jeff now despises the mailbox) yields the tax assessment statement from their City's Tax Assessor's office and they learn that their house, which was valued at $535,000 in 2006 is now worth $310,000 in 2012. Jeff smiles, identifying the only silver lining to be that a reduction in his real property taxes will kick in next year.

Because Jeff and Wendy's debt to available credit ratio tanked when Amazon Express and Bank of America eliminated their available credit – the weeks ahead see more bad news. When Jeff went to the car dealer to lease a new car, he found out his credit score had declined by over 80 points to the mid 600's. He was now considered a Class B credit risk with the result that the lease cost of the vehicle increased by $40.00 per month.

It's not quite over for the Hirsch's. Because their credit score declined due to the elimination of their available credit, Jeff noticed the interest rate on his credit card statements increased from the 6%-8% range, to an average rate of 22%! Ever diligent, Jeff called each company and requested they reconsider; pointing out to them his perfect payment history and the length of the relationship. Wendy, in the kitchen getting dinner ready heard the loud thud from the pound of Jeff's fist on his desk, followed by the slam of the phone into the receiver and a pained and loud, "Goddammit."

What can Jeff and Wendy do?

Barry and Linda – What Happened to the Good Life?

"What the hell do you expect me to do?" Holding the phone away from his ear, with eyes tensed and closed in reaction to the stress, Barry listens to the representative from Wells Fargo explain to him that unless a mortgage payment is received by Friday, they will begin foreclosure on his home. "We're sorry Mr. Baldwin, but this is what I'm required to tell you."

"We're sorry Mr. Baldwin, but this what I'm required to tell you."

Placing the receiver softly in its cradle, Barry recalls the good life – his life – his day to day, hardworking, successful life that existed each and every day for the last 10 years – until – well that's hard to say – as best as he can figure it started to end around 24 months ago and its death – well that must have already happened because there is no longer a business, he's not successful, there is no fun and Linda and he are broke.

The image of the hustle and bustle of his mortgage business floats across the back side of his eyes. He can see his people, all dressed smart and moving fast, and engaged in their efforts to close mortgage loans at Best Mortgage Company – Barry's company that had been operating for 10 years and boasted a knowledgeable staff of mortgage consultants and processors. To enhance the process even more, Barry started Best Title Company seven years ago which provided all of the title work for Best's loans and had demonstrated steady growth in the metropolitan market over the last five years beyond the boundary of Best Mortgage's deals.

Barry wasn't a one man show. Linda, his best friend and love of his life, was the community's top selling real estate agent. Linda's income alone from 2002 – 2008 was $220,000 per year.

Well – Barry muses, it's all for the history books now. Before you could wink – the cash flow evaporated. When the credit market tightened – what first became difficult quickly proceeded to impossible when it came to closing a loan. Then, poof! – the value of homes fell through the floor eliminating the demand for new mortgages and leaving the refinance market open only to the few perfect candidates who held equity in their homes and wanted and could qualify for a reduced interest rate.

In the course of only six months, Barry went from the good life to *no business* – he tried to tighten the belt and ride out the storm – first cutting back staff to bare bones, then cutting salaries and wages 30% across the board – and it might have worked except for … the bank. Barry's bank, Midtown Bank, known as a well-established commercial bank in town shifted in mid-stream – from bank and supportive of business – to "Sorry Charlie, no more tuna for you." The bank – with little fanfare – and not one iota of compassion called Best's loans and forced Barry to cease operations.

So now Barry finds himself being sued by Midtown for the unpaid balance of his business loans – which following the liquidation of the company left the bank $230,000 short. Beyond that, Midtown is the holder of a second mortgage on Barry and Linda's home and is threatening collection action on the second mortgage.

Barry, running his hand through his salt and pepper locks, sees his reflection in the picture hanging on the wall. Thoughts sprinkle by. The picture was purchased at a local art fair a couple of years back and cost $400 cash. Smiling, Barry realizes how inconsequential $400 used to be. Moving his focus back to reality, he shakes his head. Their home – their dream home –which they purchased in 2004 for $950,000 has a first mortgage to Wells Fargo for $650,000 along with the second to Midtown. The dream home today – is worth no more than $600,000.

Exasperated, Barry's thoughts turn to his problems. On his desk – lay unopened envelopes from IRS – some addressed to him and some to Linda. Wincing, in emotional pain, Barry ponders, asking himself, "What do we do now?" He knows the company did not pay its payroll taxes for the three quarters preceding the shutdown. This liability alone is $280,000, plus who knows how much in interest and penalties. On top of that, Linda, as a commissioned real estate agent was responsible for paying quarterly estimated taxes. As money dried up, however, the estimates went unpaid – while the inventory of the last sold deals in her real estate business closed, leaving her with taxable income for 2008 and $70,000 of unpaid income tax.

Hanging up the phone after speaking with his longtime friend and accountant, Barry muses, "More Good News," having found out that his combined tax liability between he and Linda is $350,000. "Boy, I'm having fun now."

Definition of Fun

1 - what provides amusement or enjoyment; **specifically:** playful often boisterous action or speech <full of **fun**>

2 - a mood for finding or making amusement <all in **fun**>

3 - a - amusement, enjoyment <sickness takes all the **fun** out of life> **b** - derisive jest : sport, ridicule <a figure of **fun**>

4 - violent or excited activity or argument

What can Barry and Linda do?

Mike and Rita –
Is this the American Dream?

Like many Americans, Mike and Rita were living the typical American way of life in 2006. They had followed the old rules – worked hard, paid their bills on time every month and had purchased the biggest house they could manage – beyond their means at the time, based upon the premise that their incomes would rise and the market value of the home would continue to increase. Rather than save money, they fueled the American economy by living off credit. Though they did not have cash in reserves, they boasted a 750 credit score and had ample available credit to cover any necessities as they presented. They were not burning up Wall Street – but life was good. They believed they were on a path to put the children through college and to live a good life with monthly net income of $7,000 per month.

Then comes November, 2008 - the real estate market crashed and their home, previously valued at $270,000, is now worth $150,000. Undaunted, Mike and Rita plowed forward. They did not realize that even when they thought things were good, they were really spending more money than they could afford because of the credit card debt they were carrying. Over the next three years, they saw their credit card balances creep up from $40,000 to $75,000, as a result of increased interest rates on the cards and increasing balances. Now – today, their cards are maxed out at $75,000 and all are carrying interest rates above 24%.

Suddenly the landscape changed. Mike and Rita now realize they have no cash in the bank, virtually no available credit to meet cash needs if they arise and the cost of servicing the credit card debt and the mortgage has made it impossible to meet their monthly budget. They cannot refinance their home to bail-out the situation and they cannot sell the home to find cash to cover their needs.

Mike and Rita are not happy. They feel lost, stressed and pessimistic about their future. What can they do?

2

Get Over It – You Need a Goal

There are a lot of angry, sad and depressed people out there. Should our friends, Rich, Jeff and Wendy, Barry and Linda and Mike and Rita feel angry? Depressed? Isolated? Guilty? Embarrassed? Probably so – most people saddled with financial crisis issues experience some if not all of these emotions. My advice, "Let's move on. *It is what it is* and it's not your fault." In fact, even if you are in part responsible due to excessive spending or use of credit – what difference does it make now? *It is what it is.*

Every day, I tell clients, friends, acquaintances and listeners, "Look to your left and look to your right at the supermarket – two of the three people are in some form of financial crisis. These are <u>not</u> the old days. These are the <u>new days</u>. Financial problems are common – they are the rule – not the exception."

The Goal

So where do we go from here? I believe the correct premise is that you must look to improve your position for the long term. To me, that means you should, to the extent possible, avoid allowing your future earnings to be saddled with paying debts of the past. I call this, *"making your money go in the bank and not to the bank."* If you put things in the proper perspective, this is precisely what large corporations do through the bankruptcy process.

I call this "making your money go in the bank and not to the bank."

These companies leave the debt behind and move forward so that their future earnings do not satisfy their past debts. In 2009, this is exactly what Chrysler and GM did with the financial backing and support of the U.S. Government. If you're chuckling to yourself and saying, "I'm not an auto company and the Feds are certainly not going to give me a bailout." – You're 100% correct! But that does not mean, however, that a similar goal and strategy can't be found to accomplish the same objective – *protect future earnings*. I believe in most situations – a strategy does exist. The key is identifying the best strategy and having the courage to implement it.

In Chrysler's and GM's case – the management of these companies sold off the assets they wanted to a new entity and left the toxic assets and debts behind. This process included negotiating down the liens of secured lenders, the retirement and healthcare benefits owed to its retirees and current employees, as well as debt to key suppliers. All the rest got nothing – nada.

How does this relate to you and me? Well, if your house is now worth $150,000, but your mortgage is $275,000 and you have $75,000 in credit card debt – your goal, just like Chrysler and GM, should be to keep the house, go forward with a mortgage of $150,000 and get rid of the credit card debt. An alternative would be to substitute your current house for one of equivalent size, value and location – so long as the mortgage or rent going forward is no greater than the fair market value of the house rather than the house that is $125,000 underwater. If you can do this, and assuming you stay away from credit cards in the future (which, in my view is staying cancer free) your future in 5 or 10 years will be remarkably different than the road it is presently headed.

Let's look at Mike and Rita. In 2006, the Fair Market Value of their house was $270,000, the balance on the Mortgage Note was $250,000 and they had $40,000 of credit card debt:

Mike and Rita's Story – 2006

▸ **FMV of Home – 2006**	$ 270,000
▸ **Mortgage**	250,000
▸ **Credit Card Debt**	40,000

Today, their home is presently worth $150,000, but the mortgage is $250,000 and they have $75,000 of credit card debt.

Mike and Rita's Story – Today

▸ **FMV of Current Home** $ 150,000

▸ **Mortgage**   250,000

▸ **Credit Card Debt**   75,000

They are struggling to break even by making minimum payments on the credit cards and holding onto the house – running one to two months behind in their mortgage payment. They are incurring late fees each month and high interest rates on their cards (24+%). If Mike and Rita are able to reduce their mortgage to the equivalent payment of the home's worth and get rid of their credit card debt, instead of falling behind each month, they would actually be able to save money for their future. Let's look at Mike and Rita's current budget:

Mike & Rita's Current Income & Expense Budget

Monthly Net Income (After Tax)	$ 7,000
Mortgage Payment	2,300
Credit Card Payments	2,625
Utilities	500
Food	1,000
Auto Expense	1,400
NET AT END OF MONTH	(825)
Everyday Quality of Life $$$	0
SAVINGS	**$ (825)**

As is simple to see – the current struggle affords no room for Quality of Life Money and worse than no savings, they are running in the red by $825 per month.

Next, let's look at the difference if we reduce the mortgage payment from a $250,000 mortgage balance to an equivalent 30 year fixed mortgage on a $150,000 home and eliminate the credit card debt:

Mike & Rita's Target Goal

	Current Struggle	Revised – Reduced Mortgage & $ –0– Credit Card Debt
Monthly Net Income (After Tax)	$ 7,000	$ 7,000
Mortgage Payment	2,300	1,525
Credit Card Payments	2,625	0
Utilities	500	500
Food	1,000	1,000
Auto Expense	1,400	1,400
NET AT END OF MONTH	(825)	2,575
Everyday Quality of Life $$$	0	(1,000)
SAVINGS	$ (825)	$ 1,575

Mike and Rita are now saving money. In fact in this example, the margin of improvement puts them positive $2,575 per month. I have, however, earmarked $1,000 as Quality of Life money since there was no quality of life in the upside down budget. Yes – life is supposed to be fun at times! There remains $1,575 savings per month. Let's assume the savings is contributed to an IRA or other form of tax deferred retirement vehicle which on a go forward basis provides an average 6% return. As to the house, let's assume market appreciation of 1% per year for the next 10 years and 2% for years 11-20 (I'm allowing real estate values to increase at a slow rate, and if you look at most experts, this rate of appreciation is considered overly optimistic).

Next, we examine where Mike and Rita will be if they allow the current struggle to continue:

Mike & Rita – Balance Sheet
Struggle Continues Forward

	Today	10 Years	20 Years
House	$ 150,000	$ 165,000	$ 198,000
Savings	0		0
Mortgage Balance	(250,000)	(214,530)	(143,248)
Credit Card Debt	(75,000)	(60,000)	(25,000)
Net Worth	$ (175,000)	$ (109,530)	$ 29,572

Mortgage – 7%, 30 Year Fixed assumed.

Credit Card – Assumption is that the short cash position will prevent Mike and Rita from discontinuing use of the cards therefore balances will not significantly decline. If the cards were not used, assuming 25% interest on the cards and payments of $2,625 per month, the balance on the cards would reduce to $-0- in 44 months

If the Current Struggle goes forward, the projection is that in 20 years, their Net Worth will be $29,572. This is not a good outcome.

Now – let's look at Mike and Rita's outcome if they are able to exit the underwater mortgage and dump the credit card debt while using the same savings assumptions listed above:

Mike & Rita – Debt Shed
Moving Forward

	Today	10 Years	20 Years
House	$ 150,000	$ 165,000	$ 198,000
Savings	0	258,109	727,714
Mortgage Balance	(150,000)	(128,719)	(85,951)
Credit Card Debt	0	0	0
Net Worth	$ 0	$ 294,390	$ 839,763

Savings assumed at $1,575 per month in tax deferred
retirement account with a 6% return

The results are life changing! Moving forward they are allowed $1,000 for Quality of Life spending – and even then, at the end of 20 years, the net worth accumulation is $839,763 compared to $29,572!

> **Putting cash in the bank rather than paying off debt long term is critical.**

Can there be any question what Mike and Rita must do? You can put aside all of the obstacles if they exist. Suppose if Mike and Rita were sitting in my office today and asked, will doing this ruin my credit? In their case, my answer would be, "No, your credit has already been severely damaged by your history of late payments." But suppose Mike and Rita's situation was virtually identical and they had never been late on a payment, had perfect credit histories with FICO scores of 750? In that case, my answer would be, "Yes, the go forward plan will harm your credit score for some time, but over time the problem will vanish. Would you rather have a perfect credit score every day for the next 20 years and have a net worth of $30,000 at the end or would you prefer to take a "hit" on your credit score and in 20 years have a net worth in excessive of $840,000?" The concern over the impact on one's credit score, while legitimate, is far over played. You are not better off in 20 years with a perfect credit score and a measly $30,000 net worth.

Would you rather have a perfect credit score every day for the next 20 years and have a net worth of $30,000 at the end or would you prefer to take a "hit" on your credit score and in 20 years have a net worth in excessive of $840,000?

IT'S NOT ABOUT YOUR CREDIT SCORE.

SAVINGS ACCUMULATION IS MORE IMPORTANT THAN YOUR CREDIT SCORE.

What about other obstacles? Will I be able to get financing to buy a car? The answer is yes, but, in the beginning, there might be a cost. If you have "subprime credit" you may have to pay a premium interest rate for the loan. That thought is distasteful, but you have to look at the big picture. In exchange for the inconvenience of paying a premium rate on a car loan for a couple of years, you are gaining the benefit of saving the money you've gained by having shed the credit card debt and excessive mortgage costs. Also, keep in mind, in Mike and Rita's case (like many people) they already have subprime credit so this isn't even an obstacle.

The goal should be clear to you. If it is not – you need to re-read this section and make sure you've absorbed the enormity of the issue and your goal.

IF YOU DUMP YOUR DEBT, YOUR FUTURE IS BRIGHT.

On the flip side – if you do not shed the debt, your only chance to recoup what you've lost in the Financial Crisis is to earn more money than you ever did before. Worse yet – if you do that, the majority of that money will only serve to satisfy your creditors – not you or your family.

Now that you have a fix on what the goal is, as well as the dramatic positive benefits to be realized by it, you need to get excited. Getting there will not be pain free. For most - the pain is nominal. Far more significant is the pain and misery you may have already endured, as well as the pain and misery you're certain to endure in the future unless you take action.

With the goal implanted within you, let's explore the tools that are available to accomplish the task.

The Tools
of
Financial Crisis Management

There are a number of tools at play when it comes to the goal of shedding debt. In the housing sector, we have "foreclosure," "short sales," and "loan modifications." In resolving credit card debt, we have "debt settlement" or "debt resolution" as I like to call it. The tools used depend on the task and the circumstances. A carpenter will sometimes purchase 2" x 6"s, cut them to size and affix them to drywall. Next the drywall is sanded, followed by a molding with paint or a cover to finish. Sometimes, however, a different mix of tasks and tools are needed for a particular job. In an office setting, walls are often pre-fabricated and metal studs are used instead of wood. Thus, a different process and mix of tools are used.

The process of shedding debt is no different. It is a process and the specific circumstances you face will dictate the order and mix of tools employed to accomplish the task.

So how familiar and how much do you need to know about the tools? I believe you need to know the basics – as to how the tool is used and what it can accomplish. By analogy, a carpenter needs to know what type of situation is correct to use a circle saw and how to use it. It is not necessary for him to understand the history, physical composition and manufacturing process of the particular saw. My goal is for you to understand the use and process of the "tools" – without boring or exhausting you with historical detail or excessive and useless information.

So, let's open the tool box and see what we have:

The Tools

Foreclosure	*The Bankruptcy Laws*
Short Sale	*Debt Resolution*
Loan Modification	*Tax Relief*

3

Foreclosure

I hope you're asking – why is "foreclosure" listed as a "tool?" Foreclosure is the process by which the lender takes the property back from the homeowner or forces the property to be sold at auction to the highest bidder thereby causing the homeowner to lose their home. So how can this be a tool? The answer is depending on your situation and the state you live in – the best strategy with regard to your underwater house is sometimes not to keep the house. If the mortgage far exceeds the market value of the house and the lender will not modify the mortgage so that the principal of the mortgage loan is approximate to the house's value, you are smarter to get rid of the house and the mortgage and replace it with a house equal in size and personal appeal, but at the current market value.

VIEW YOUR HOUSE AS AN IMPORTANT ASSET – NOT AS YOUR LIFE ITSELF.

THE HOUSE IS NOT THE HOME.

Your "home" is the abode you live in. It includes the memories, the people, the energy of family and, of course, emotion. Your "house" is the physical asset, the structure which you own and which you have likely pledged to a mortgage lender to secure payment of the funds borrowed to purchase the home or for other expenses arising from a home equity loan. If you are presently underwater on your house (for whatever the reason) – a valid goal is to move your "home" to a different site and leave the "house" that is underwater. For some, this is a difficult coin to swallow. If, however, your situation is similar to Mike and Rita's then the correct conclusion is self-evident. Staying in a house that is way underwater is throwing away your chance to accumulate savings for retirement.

Additionally, there are many people who are presently living in houses with mortgages that they just can no longer afford for a variety of reasons. They may have stepped too high up the ladder with a no-doc, low or no-interest adjustable loan while riding the market bubble, or they may have incurred an income loss due to job cuts or a business failure. The practical reality is that you need to be in a home with a mortgage payment you can afford that allows some savings for the future. Though in the past, an argument could be made that savings and growth will come from the appreciation in market values, that argument holds little, if any, water in the present and foreseeable future climate. The reality is that there is no point in attempting to modify a loan if the gap is too wide. We must all face the facts and the music in certain respects. The 1990's and 2000's were a time when America rode the RECC bubble. The what? The Real Estate Credit Card ("RECC") bubble! RECC is my acronym for what we now have left - which is the Train-RECC! During this twenty year period, no doc loans (no documentation to justify the borrower's ability to repay the loan) flourished, as well as interest only, subprime lending, 125% loan to value financing and the rest of the wild gizmos that made it so easy to purchase or build a home – even if you could not afford to pay for it. On top of that, if you had a track record of paying your bills on time, it was easy to obtain anywhere from $25,000 to $200,000 of available credit on credit cards.

The 1990's and 2000's were a time when America rode the RECC bubble. The what? The Real Estate Credit Card ("RECC") bubble! RECC is my acronym for what we now have left - which is the Train-RECC!

The RECC bubble created incentives for people to buy houses in excess of what their income allowed. The expectation was that the house could be refinanced to cover any shortfalls or if necessary, flipped at a hefty profit – with the profit rolled into the next home – allowing the homeowner to enjoy a nicer home and bigger asset with a mortgage that was affordable. It was a nice concept and worked for a while for many people. Unfortunately, we now know that the concept failed.

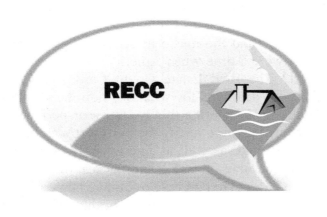

We may not have known it then, but we certainly know it now. The RECC bubble has burst and all that we have left is the "reccage." The wake of the fallout is far bigger than anyone would have imagined. Industries such as residential and commercial development have been destroyed. A builder simply cannot build a house that is price competitive with the depressed property values for existing homes and the continuing and ever looming foreclosure inventory.

The important point here is to learn from the past. Going forward, your goal should be to acquire a house that you can afford to pay for and maintain. The days of 10% annual increases in value are gone. It is simply not realistic to think we are going to reinvent the bubble and then ride it again in the near future. America as a country does learn from its mistakes. In this case, governmental oversight and regulation designed to protect against the RECC and debacle also means there should be no reasonable expectation of sustained super price escalation on a wide spread basis.

The Foreclosure Process

Before we get started, let me explain the foreclosure process. Foreclosure is the process by which a lender that holds a mortgage or in some states, a deed of trust, seeks to sell the house and apply the proceeds from the sale to satisfy all or a part of the debt owed by the owner to the lender. So before we talk about foreclosure, you need a house or other real property owned by you. You have borrowed money from a lender and have agreed to pledge the real property as collateral to secure the lender's repayment. The "pledge" is in the form of a mortgage or deed of trust. Going forward, I'll just refer to it as a "mortgage."

When you borrow the money from the lender, you typically, sign and give the lender a Mortgage Note. The Mortgage Note is a promissory note that represents your monetary obligation. Going forward, I'll call the Mortgage Note, the "Note." The mortgage is the security or pledge of the real property itself. When a person defaults in paying, we often say he or she is behind on the mortgage. Such an expression, though readily understood to mean the borrower has missed payments due the lender, is not technically correct. In actuality, the person is behind or in default in making the payment required by the Note. The lender then, in accordance with its rights under the Note and the mortgage, can declare the Note in "default." The default then triggers the lender's remedies and options it may pursue to enforce payment of the debt.

When the lender declares the "default" it does so by sending written notice to the person or persons who signed the Note. (When you sign the Note, you are the borrower and mortgagor, and you are also called the "maker" of the Note). In that notice, the lender informs the person that because the payment was missed, the lender is "accelerating" the required payment of the Note such that the entire principal balance, plus all accrued interest, as well as late fees and attorney fees becomes immediately due.

At this point, the lender has options as to the method it seeks to enforce payment. The lender can simply ignore the real property pledged by the mortgage and sue the persons who signed the note in state court to obtain a money judgment for the unpaid debt. The lender, once reducing its claim to a judgment, seeks to enforce payment by attempting to seize property, levying on bank accounts of the person or garnishing their wages through a wage garnishment served on their employer.

Rather than sue on the Note, the lender can foreclose the mortgage. When the lender holds a mortgage, foreclosure of the mortgage has historically been a much easier remedy to pursue collection of the debt. Foreclosure is a remedy controlled by the laws of each particular state so the exact process varies from state to state. For our purposes, there are a couple of distinctions you should understand, as well as a couple of key common elements that are important.

Foreclosure by Advertisement or Nonjudicial Foreclosure is the common form of foreclosure pursued by a lender. Twenty-nine states permit Nonjudicial Foreclosure. It works typically like this. The lender publishes a foreclosure notice in the legal newspaper that covers the county where the property is located. The publication notice establishes a "sale date" or "auction date" for the property, includes the legal description of the property and the amount of the indebtedness to the lender that is presently outstanding. The sale is usually conducted by the county sheriff at a designated location – often times the county courthouse. At the sale, the highest bidder for the property receives a "Sheriff's Deed" to the property entitling the winning bidder to ownership of the property subject to certain limitations or redemption rights depending on the state's foreclosure law. More often than not, the only person who appears at the auction is the lender. Since the lender is owed the debt, the lender can bid up to the amount of the total unpaid indebtedness without having to tender any money since it is the lender who is owed the money. Other bidders must actually tender the funds for the awarded bid price at the sale.

In many states that permit Nonjudicial Foreclosure (i.e. foreclosure by advertisement) after the sale date, the foreclosed owner has a "Statutory Redemption Period" which allows the foreclosed owner to retain possession of the property for a period ranging from 3 months to one year depending on how much of the original loan was paid prior to the default. Some states laws, however, such as Colorado, Georgia, Montana, Nevada, New Hampshire and Washington do not provide a redemption period. In those states that do provide a redemption period, the right to possession terminates if the property is abandoned by the owner and in some states if the property is farm land, the redemption period is longer. During the "Statutory Redemption Period," the foreclosed owner can also "redeem" the property by paying the amount of the bid price at the auction, plus costs, insurance and accrued interest from the sale date. By way of example, the typical redemption period in Michigan is 6 months, in Minnesota it is 6 months, and in Illinois and Maine it is 90 days.

In the states in which there is no post sale/auction redemption period, the borrower is typically provided an opportunity to retain the property but the period is referred to as the "Equity of Redemption Period" and runs from the time the lender declares the default up to the date of sale. Here the borrower can redeem and avoid the sale by paying off the accelerated balance before the sale date. Most mortgages and state laws also provide that the borrower can reinstate the mortgage by paying all payments in arrears, plus costs, including lender attorney fees, so long as the payment is made prior to the foreclosure sale. The redemption remedy (both statutory and equitable) and reinstatement remedy sound better than in actuality because people facing foreclosure are not typically in a cash position to tender the necessary money and their disadvantaged position makes it virtually impossible to borrow money.

In addition to Nonjudicial Foreclosure, the lender can also pursue what is referred to as "Judicial Foreclosure," which functionally accomplishes the same objective but differs in that the lender must actually commence a lawsuit in state court to gain the necessary authority to sell the property and dispossess the owner from possession. Nineteen states, such as Florida, Connecticut, Delaware and South Carolina do not permit

Nonjudicial Foreclosure and only allow Judicial Foreclosure. For purposes of our discussion, the distinction between judicial versus nonjudicial has little significance.

Another key state law question relating to foreclosure is whether the lenders are permitted to foreclosure and thereafter pursue a deficiency claim against you for the difference between the amount owed on the Note compared to market value of the property at the time of foreclosure. The vast majority of jurisdictions allow the lender to pursue the deficiency. According to *RealtyTrac©*, there are 12 states that have "Anti-Deficiency or Non-Recourse" provisions in their foreclosure laws – Alaska, Arizona, California, Connecticut, Florida, Idaho, Minnesota, North Carolina, North Dakota, Texas, Utah and Washington. The non-recourse provisions do not typically apply to home equity, HELOC or junior mortgages.

> **IMPORTANT**
>
> Without question, you need to know the particular laws of your state as to the foreclosure process when formulating the Financial Crisis Management strategy. It is important because we first need to know if the plan has to address the possibility of a deficiency claim (if you are in a recourse state) and often we utilize the period encompassing the foreclosure process (both pre and post-sale) to negotiate with the lender and to build cash reserves if the plan calls for strategically not making the mortgage payment.

So let's summarize. The lender holds a mortgage on your property which is a pledge of the property as security for repayment of the Note you sign when you borrow the money to purchase or refinance the property. The lender has two remedies it can pursue when you fail to pay. It can sue on the Note or it can foreclose.

Let's examine how the process unfolds from the lender's and owner's perspective. If the lender forecloses on the house and bids at the sale the amount of the unpaid balance on the Note, the debt is extinguished. Such a bid is commonly called a "full-credit bid." In this case, the debt is satisfied because the bid price equaled the unpaid debt. There is no shortfall in this situation and no exposure of being sued by the lender for the difference between the unpaid balance on the Note and the value of the property as of the date of the auction sale. On the other hand, if the lender is the only purchaser (bidder) at the auction sale and bids less than the amount of the debt and *you are not in a "Anti-Deficiency" or "Non-Recourse State,"* the lender can pursue a claim against the foreclosed owner for the deficiency – the difference between the price bid by the lender and the unpaid balance on the Note. To preserve this claim, the lender normally has a market value appraisal of the property conducted in close proximity to the auction sale and then bids a price equal to the appraised value at the auction sale. The lender can then attempt to collect this deficiency by filing a lawsuit in state court against the foreclosed owner seeking a judgment for the deficiency.

Deeds in Lieu of Foreclosure and Short Sales coupled with a release from the lender are methods by which homeowners seek to shed themselves of the underwater house but at the same time eliminate the potential exposure of a deficiency claim being pursued against them by the lender. If, however, the market value of the home is in close proximity to the unpaid Note balance, the bid price by the lender will typically extinguish the debt secured by the first mortgage. In that case, the concern of exposure from a claim for the deficiency is not significant. In anti-deficiency or non-recourse states, this is typically a non-issue as to the first mortgage, but as stated, you need to be specific as to your state's foreclosure law in making this assumption or assessment.

From a planning perspective, we have to evaluate the risk and likelihood that a lender, in foreclosing on the house, will seek to pursue a deficiency claim. A major distinction exists between the lender holding the first mortgage compared to lenders holding home equity and other second and junior mortgages.

When you have a second or multiple mortgages, the pledge to the lender holding the second or later mortgage provides far less protection to the lender given the depressed real estate market of today where property values have dipped so low that the market value of the homes is consistently less than the first mortgage and certainly inadequate to cover both or all of the mortgages. The mortgage lenders receive their priority based on when the mortgages are recorded and issued. Second and third mortgages are often called "junior mortgages" or "junior liens." A home equity lien or HELOC is simply a mortgage and assuming it is in a second or lesser priority position to a first mortgage, it is a junior mortgage or junior lien.

To understand the process and anticipated responses you will receive from the lenders holding junior mortgages, it is helpful to understand the rights of the junior mortgage lender compared to the rights of the first mortgage lender. When a first mortgage is foreclosed, the property will be sold to the highest bidder. If the sale price is equal to or greater than the amount of the unpaid Note secured by the first mortgage, the excess would flow to junior mortgage lenders according to their priority. For example, assume the balance on the Note secured by the first mortgage is $200,000, and the balance on the Note for the second mortgage is $50,000 and there is also a third mortgage and Note for $20,000. If the bid at the auction on the foreclosure of the first mortgage is $260,000, then $200,000 goes to payoff the first mortgage lender, the second mortgage lender gets the next $50,000 and the third mortgage lender gets the remaining $10,000. In this instance, the only exposure left for the foreclosed borrower is a suit from the third mortgage lender which only received $10,000 against the $20,000 balance. A result such as this, however, in the current market, rarely occurs because the property value is typically less than the first mortgage.

In today's world, a common example is that you have the same $200,000, $50,000 and $20,000 mortgages, but the value of the property as of the foreclosure sale is $200,000 or slightly less. Typically, the bidder at the sale is the first mortgage lender and it will bid the unpaid balance it is owed (or less if it intends to pursue a deficiency). This means, if the second mortgage lender or any other junior mortgage lender wishes to protect its interest in the security value of the property, they have to purchase the property at the foreclosure sale which requires them to tender cash equal to the first mortgage lender's balance and any other liens having priority to their lien (i.e. if the third mortgage lender wants to protect itself, it must tender cash to take out the first two mortgage lenders). The junior lender who purchases at the foreclosure sale must then wait to regain possession of the property for any applicable redemption period to run – which then requires that the borrower vacate the property. After that occurs, it then must reclaim the property, repair the property and ultimately sell the property for more than the amount it has paid at the auction sale, plus holding costs and repairs in order to realize *any* money against the original unpaid balance of the junior mortgage note. Needless to say, in contrast to the holder of the first mortgage, junior mortgage lenders have a difficult road to follow in order to recoup the loss exposure on a junior mortgage note.

The junior mortgage lender's difficult road has consequences. In the quest to shed debt and rid oneself of a house that is underwater you will find junior lenders are more difficult to deal with because they are not positioned to recover any money from the sale of the property. The distinction is that it is easier for the first mortgage lender to take a partial loss on the transaction and forego chasing the owner of the deficiency compared to the junior mortgage lender agreeing to receive nothing. Bottom line here – the junior mortgage lender is not going to give up its claim for nothing. Keep in mind, the junior mortgage lenders are not in a position to receive anything from the sale of the property because the first lender will receive those proceeds. The junior mortgage lenders, can, however, as we've discussed, sue you as the borrower for the unpaid balance on their Note.

Foreclosure as a Tool

Now that you have a basic understanding of the foreclosure process and the varied interests of the players, let's identify how "foreclosure" is a tool in Financial Crisis Management. Here's how. If your house is way underwater, the goal is not to modify the mortgage loan. The goal is to "shed the debt" which means get rid of the house and the Note obligation. Next, you need to find a new house that is similar in style or otherwise meets your needs and that house is priced at current market value – whether to rent or purchase. Now, assume in the situation just discussed, the property's fair market value is equal to the first mortgage and there are two junior mortgages. If you qualify, we can file a Chapter 7 bankruptcy and discharge your monetary obligation under all of the mortgage notes. We then proceed to allow foreclosure of the first mortgage because it allows you to live in the house without cost (other than utilities and insurance to cover your contents and liability exposure) for a sustained period preceding foreclosure, during the foreclosure process and during the redemption period. I often call this, "Getting Your Equity Out."

Suppose your mortgage payment was $2,500 per month and you purchased a $300,000 home with 10% down and a $270,000 mortgage. Assume now, the house is only worth $200,000. Well – obviously you have no equity in this home since its $70,000 underwater on the mortgage and you're $100,000 short from the value when you purchased it. Nevertheless, when you purchased it originally, before the Financial Crisis, you had $30,000 of equity represented by your down payment. "Getting Your Equity Out," when I use these words, really means saving the money represented by the mortgage payments you are not making throughout the foreclosure process. A twelve month period, in most states, is likely from start to finish. In this instance, 12 months x $2,500 = $30,000 – the equity you lost in the crisis.

Of course – the banks and probably the government would not like the gloss in this analysis, but two things must be kept in mind. First, no one is knocking on your door to help you. Second, the loss you've incurred is real and just as the banks and major businesses are taking steps to insure their recovery – you need to do the same. Now, I recognize, in many situations the homeowner (technically, I prefer *"houseowner"*) has suffered an income decline due to job loss or business failure and in that case, the mortgage payments that are not paid to the lender will not be saved because the money is simply not there. But remember, we're talking tools here. In the case of a person who is underwater in their house, in the right situation, foreclosure can be a tool to allow them to exit from the house obligation to the lender *and provide a means to save money for a future purchase or lease with an option to purchase* a new house or other investment.

4

The Short Sale

When you give a mortgage on your property, you are granting the lender a lien on the property that can be discharged or satisfied in only three ways. One way is to pay the lender the full amount due on the Note the mortgage secures. In a sale situation, a payoff letter is ordered by the title company handling the closing and from the proceeds paid by the Purchaser; the amount due the lender is set aside and paid to it in exchange for the lender's discharge of the mortgage. Other than paying the lender off in full, the second way to obtain a discharge of the mortgage is to obtain the lender's consent to discharge its mortgage without payment or with a payment less than the amount owed by the lender. The third way to obtain a discharge is to "lien strip" the lender's mortgage in a Chapter 13 Bankruptcy case. Lien Stripping is a great tool we use in Chapter 13 bankruptcies, but it only applies to junior mortgages where there is no equity attaching to the junior mortgage. We'll discuss this later when we review the Bankruptcy Tools.

A "short sale" is the situation where a lender consents to discharge its mortgage without regard to the payment amount it receives. This means the property (typically a residential home) is sold for less than the outstanding balance owed on the mortgages of the property. A short sale can only occur with the consent of the mortgage company that is not receiving full payment of the balance it is owed. The lender's consent allows the property to be sold and the lender releases its mortgage lien against the property. Without the release, the seller cannot convey clear title to the purchaser because of the mortgage lien.

There are a couple of issues in play here. First, the terms of the lender's consent are controlled by the lender. The lender will issue a letter indicating the terms by which it will agree to release its lien for less than the amount owed. This letter typically spells out conditions that must be satisfied, including the amount of proceeds to be paid by the lender, warranties and representations from the owner of the property designed to prohibit any form of collusion between the seller and purchaser from the lender's perspective. In order to gain the benefit of the short sale, there must be compliance with the specified terms of the lender's approval letter.

A critical component in any short sale is whether the lender is agreeing to release its remaining claim against the mortgage holder of the Note. *This is often assumed to be the case – but it is not something you can assume.* In any situation where a Short Sale is in play, the borrower who is seeking to have the mortgage and debt discharged must be sure it is clearly spelled out in writing that the discharge of the mortgage is also a release of any claim by the lender on the Note. You cannot believe the real estate salesperson, the title company processor or the representative of the lender. You must verify this fact in writing! *I repeat, you must verify this fact in writing!* Many of the lenders have standard form approval letters which they will not vary. These letters must be scrutinized carefully to insure that they provide for a cancelation of the deficiency. The written word is gold in real estate transactions so if the approval letter does not provide for release of the deficiency – you, as the seller/borrower, should refuse to close on the transaction until adequate written assurance is provided.

Let's focus now on the process. The process is different when the person agreeing to the short sale is the holder of a first mortgage compared to a junior mortgage holder. In some markets, a lender holding the first mortgage will not consider granting its consent to a short sale unless the property has been actively marketed for two to three months. The reasoning is that the lender is seeking to assure itself that the price being paid for the home is the market price. The lender is trying to make sure the property is not being sold for less than what it could or should be sold. If you think about it, this makes sense. The lender is not agreeing to take less than it is owed because they are "nice," "committed to the community" or any other social cause. They are doing so, only because they recognize that it is economically in their interest to have the mortgage holder market and find a buyer for the property at the best price attainable rather than to go through the time, cost and risk to the property that arises when the property is foreclosed. In this connection, in addition to the requirement that the property is on the market, most lenders will not give consideration to accepting a short sale unless the homeowner is behind on the payments – which acts to demonstrate to the lender that there is a substantial risk of foreclosure if the short sale is not accepted.

Junior mortgages are a bit different. The interest of the junior mortgage holder is dependent upon the market value of the home compared to the first mortgage. If the market value of the home is less than the first mortgage, the junior mortgage holder is in a position where it will realize no money upon the foreclosure of the home by the first lender or by the junior lender. The reason is that the proceeds of the sale, after selling costs, will ultimately go toward satisfying a portion of the first mortgage holder's lien. The junior mortgage holder, in this instance, can play the role of the obstructionist. Remember – the mortgage holder, whether first or junior, does not have to consent to release its lien unless it is paid in full.

In the short sale, the first mortgage holder agrees to release its lien for less than it is owed (we call this "going short" or a "short pay") because it is getting what it believes to be the realistic proceeds from the sale of the property at market value – and it in fact will do worse, not better, if it elects to foreclose. The junior mortgage holder, however, is not going to get anything out of the sale because the proposed purchase will not cover the first mortgage. So, will the junior mortgage holder release its lien for nothing since it is not in a position to gain from a foreclosure? The answer is that it could, but it typically will not. Instead, the junior mortgage holder will typically obstruct the sale by refusing to release its lien unless it is paid something – typically an amount in the range of $2,000 to $5,000. Here, the junior mortgage holder is interfering with the desired outcome of three parties – the seller, the purchaser and the first mortgage holder, as well as the real estate brokers who have worked to put the deal together. The junior mortgage holder uses its role and power as an obstructionist to effectively demand money for the release of its lien. Keep in mind; it is within the power of the junior mortgage holder to kill the entire deal. The normal outcome in this situation is that the release fee required by the junior lienholder is paid from the proceeds of the sale (thereby reducing the amount received by the first mortgage lender). Sometimes the situation is more difficult and numerous calls and emails between the brokers, the first mortgage holders, the seller and the purchaser are required in order to amass enough funds from some or all of the parties to satisfy the demand of the junior mortgage holder so that its discharge of the mortgage is obtained.

There are many issues in play in this situation. The junior lienholder may be a commercial bank or mortgage lender that is participating in the HAMP program or programs falling within the purview of Fannie Mae and Freddie Mac as to first mortgages. In this situation, the procedures employed by the junior lien holder are more defined and there is a process that ensues in order to gain the release. Junior liens, however, are sometimes liens pledged to commercial and private lending sources to support business loans. In this setting, the lender is not bound by any government programs and the range of negotiations and positions taken by the lenders varies greatly – which typically then requires greater effort and creativity to accomplish the goal of gaining the release.

Liens that are junior to the first mortgage also arise in the form of tax liens filed by IRS and state governments against the taxpayer as well as construction liens filed against the property by contractors in accordance with state law. Many people are misinformed on tax liens – having been told that the existence of a tax lien precludes the possibility of successfully short selling the property. This is not correct. Where there is no equity attaching to the lien, IRS has a defined policy and procedure to apply for a release of the lien as do most state taxing authorities. To do so, you are well advised to engage the services of an attorney or CPA that is experienced in this process. Short sales need to move quickly so you do not want to lose the buyer or have your lender's approval expire due to inexperience in handling the lien release process with the taxing authorities.

Many people are misinformed on tax liens – having been told that the existence of a tax lien precludes the possibility of successfully short selling the property. This is not correct. Where there is no equity attaching to the lien, IRS has a defined policy and procedure to apply for a release of the lien as do most state taxing authorities.

Construction liens are a different animal. In this situation, negotiations have to ensue with the lien holder to obtain the release. The lien holder does not have to agree to discharge simply because there is no equity. In this scenario, the lien holder is typically looking for a resolution of the entire claim – so there will be a need for more sophisticated negotiation on the borrower's behalf in order to accomplish the task. As a preliminary matter, you should investigate whether the lien is valid under state law. States have specific procedural requirements in order to file and prosecute construction liens. It is not unusual for a construction lien to be recorded against property in situations where the lien claimant has not complied with the statutory requirements. If you can determine the lien is invalid or is subject to challenge as to its validity, your bargaining position to gain the release will be significantly enhanced.

Will the junior mortgage holder also agree to release the owner (the "seller") from the remaining monetary obligation on the Note secured by the second mortgage? Here the answer is "sometimes." On the "no" side, the reason is that the bargain struck with the junior mortgage holder is a payment of a nominal sum in exchange for its release of its lien – not for the discharge of the remaining debt. The junior mortgage holder retains its right to pursue collection of the remaining balance on its Note from the owner. If you are in this situation, you need to know that you will have to address the possible claim of the junior mortgage holder at a later stage – in a manner similar with other debts you have such as credit card debt, student loans, etc. Keep in mind, this is expected in the context of the overall strategies that exist for shedding debt. You can only accomplish so much in certain transactions and at certain times. In the short sale setting, if you shed the first mortgage obligation and the first mortgage lender has released you from any remaining debt then you have accomplished a lot toward the master plan. As to the junior mortgage holder that used its position to get some money, but has not discharged your debt, we'll use other tools to address that issue.

Opportunities to settle on the deficiency with the junior lien holder as part of the short sale *sometimes do arise.* If the junior lienholder is also the first lienholder (common in the "piggyback mortgage" situation where the initial loan was structured as a first and second mortgage), the lender is participating in the government HAMP program or the first mortgage is held by Fannie Mae or Freddie Mac, there often exists opportunity to gain a release of any claim of deficiency on the second. The release is negotiated and the borrower reaches terms where payment of funds are paid to the second lienholder in exchange for the release of the deficiency claim in addition to that which the lender receives to discharge the mortgage. In certain limited circumstances, the second lienholder is actually precluded from receiving additional funds and the discharge of the lien and the deficiency claim are dictated by the applicable (and ever changing) government program.

It is therefore important that you investigate this issue in the context of your short sale. Keep in mind, the release of the deficiency is collateral to the sale transaction. The broker, buyer and lien holders will not be advocating on your behalf on this issue. They are all in a position to economically benefit by merely making sure the deal "closes" which means the release of the liens are obtained. The person you engage to represent you on the short sale should be your advocate on this issue. You need to make sure every effort is made to gain the release of the deficiency from the first mortgage holder and any junior mortgage holders. In my experience, I find that too often the person engaged to represent the borrower/seller on the short sale is tied to the desire to close the real estate transaction and is therefore lacking the motivation to aggressively seek the release of the deficiency on your behalf. Such a circumstance arises when the so-called "short sale expert" is also the broker or any person (attorney included) who is compensated from the proceeds of the sale. At first blush, this may seem beneficial since you save the cost of paying the short sale expert because it is paid from the lender's proceeds at the sale. I disagree, however. Shedding the debt is the paramount goal of the short sale and you are better off engaging an attorney whose role is to accomplish that goal only. As long as the cost charged is reasonable, the investment in ad independent advocate is a smart move in pursuing the critical goal of eliminating the deficiency.

When we handle a short sale, we are not paid from the proceeds of the sale. First – it's annoying to the lender to see that additional money is being taken from the sale. More importantly, if the transaction is about to close except the lenders are demanding too much money be paid to them by the borrower (from the borrower's own funds) in order to release the remaining deficiency, we, as the attorneys, refuse to close the transaction as a means of pushing everyone – the lender, the brokers and the buyer – to apply pressure on the lender and if necessary to kick in the necessary dollars in order to gain a complete release or better deal. If your advocate is getting paid only if the deal closes – then you have created a scenario where their financial interest is in conflict with yours. Such a move should be avoided. Remember your goal - and make sure your professionals are aligned to accomplish the task.

5

Deed in Lieu of Foreclosure

When a homeowner is facing foreclosure, a consensual closure to the process can sometimes be obtained if the homeowner is willing to surrender their interest in the property to the foreclosing lender and the lender is willing to accept their deed to the property in satisfaction of any further obligation from the owner. This is known as giving a "deed in lieu of foreclosure." The lender avoids the costs and risks akin to the foreclosure process by accepting the property from the owner. In virtually all circumstances, the lender, in accepting the deed in lieu of foreclosure is doing so with the understanding that the tender of the deed will satisfy any further obligation that the owner owes the lender. Caution is still needed here, however, because what people say to each other does not govern – it is what the written documents state. The only way to be certain that the lender, in accepting the deed in lieu of foreclosure, is releasing the homeowner from any further obligation on the debt is to make sure the lender's obligation is reduced to writing in a binding agreement. The last person you can trust is the lender and worse yet, the statements made by the lender's representative that is pushing the paperwork for your deal along with 1,000 other pending matters. Common sense dictates that you should have this agreement reviewed by an attorney so that you are certain your obligations on the mortgage loan are being extinguished. Such agreements are short form documents and the cost of obtaining this confirmation should be nominal.

The deed in lieu accomplishes the "shed the debt" goal of the first mortgage. It also provides certainty. As discussed, if the foreclosure process goes forward to sale, you have risk that the lender will bid less than the outstanding balance of the unpaid mortgage loan which presents the potential that you could be sued down the road by the lender for a deficiency claim. The Deed in Lieu puts this issue to bed as between you and the first lender. On the flip side, you will most likely have to surrender possession of the property at an earlier date and the release of any claims by the lender against you will be conditioned upon your surrender of the premises without unduly causing damage to the property. As is discussed in the next chapter on Loan Modifications, under the HAMP program there are provisions in the Home Affordable Foreclosure Alternatives ("HAFA") program for homeowners who do not qualify for a Loan Modification to receive compensation for their cooperation in concluding a Deed in Lieu arrangement and the lender also receives compensation under the program.

Just like in a short sale, you cannot conclude a deed in lieu unless the junior mortgage holders discharge their mortgage liens. Under the HAMP Participating Agreement, servicers holding junior mortgages are required, in some circumstances, to discharge their liens.

Keep in mind – a "discharge of the lien or mortgage" eliminates the impediment to concluding the short sale or the deed in lieu, but it is NOT a release of the claim of indebtedness on the Note to the junior mortgage lender. There is *no release* unless that is specifically provided for. If, at the time you are concluding a short sale or deed in lieu, you are dealing with a junior mortgage holder to obtain its discharge, you should certainly ask for a release of the underlying indebtedness as well. There is no law against asking! More likely than not they will not grant the release to you, but you should request it. The junior mortgage lender may be willing to accept a small payment in full satisfaction of the debt. We always ask for the release on behalf of our clients and also do our utmost to convince the lender that a bankruptcy filing is inevitable for our client (*we engage in spirited bluffing here at times!*). Once the lender realizes that the future holds virtually no possible hope of recovery, it is much easier to negotiate a small dollar settlement to do away with the junior liens.

At the time you conclude a short sale or deed in lieu it is certainly possible that you will not be successful in obtaining a complete release of the money obligation owed to the junior lienholder. Don't panic. You will have numerous additional opportunities to deal with the obligation. The claim of the junior lenders is not going to be a surprise to you. Financial Crisis Management is about handling and managing issues and following a strategy. The existence of the claim of the junior lenders is not going to appear as a surprise that derails your plan. When the opportunities best present themselves is when you address them.

When I explain this to a client, I call it the "backup plan." For each desired strategy, there is a backup plan that yields a solution if the preferred and simplest solution is not available. Financial Crisis Management is not a static set of rules and outcomes. It is important to adopt a pragmatic approach to the process. You start with the goal and you continue on a path seeking that outcome.

Financial Crisis Management is not a static set of rules and outcomes. It is important to adopt a pragmatic approach to the process. You start with the goal and you continue on a path seeking that outcome.

There are some risks along the way, but the key to covering those risks is to be sure that you have Plan B and Plan C back-up plans on hand in case they are needed. A simple example exists in the short sale and deed in lieu situation as to the junior lienholder. Plan A says, let's ask for a complete release of the lien *and the debt.* If the lender agrees, great! If not, the Plan B back up plan is to proceed forward and then negotiate a settlement of the deficiency claim down the road. As long as you have mapped out the plan, you simply need to stay the course. If the Plan B back-up plan is not successful, a Plan C back-up plan might call for the commencement of a Chapter 13 Bankruptcy. In practice, I find that it is unusual to resort to a Plan C back-up plan. Nevertheless, having the back-up plan is critical so that you are not walking forward in the dark and you minimize uncertainty and anxiety in the execution of your strategy.

6

The Loan Modification

The buzz words of 2009 – "I need a loan mod." How about this one – "We guaranty we'll cut your payment in half or we'll give you your money back." As in every event of major economic proportion, new businesses emerge in an effort to take advantage of the market conditions. After all – we do have a capitalist system designed to reward creativity with profit. Unfortunately, as is often the case, the floodgates of opportunity often give way to slipshod business practices where the dollar is chased by the unscrupulous in exchange for promises that cannot be fulfilled. Such has been the case with the proliferation of loan modification, tax relief and debt settlement companies which employ large national advertising budgets to create the impression of professionalism and competence, but, practically speaking, offer at best nothing more than exorbitant fees for non-attentive and sloppy paper pushing and, at worst, businesses that charge high upfront fees and vanish overnight without providing any service or returning fees for unfulfilled services.

Unfortunately, as is often the case, the floodgates of opportunity often give way to slipshod business practices where the dollar is chased by the unscrupulous in exchange for promises that cannot be fulfilled.

So is there anything legitimate about loan modifications and how they are used as a tool in Financial Crisis Management? The answer is yes – a loan modification is often a valid undertaking and it plays an important role is the process. By definition, a Loan Modification is an agreement between the mortgage holder (normally the lender or mortgage company) and the borrower (typically, the property owner) wherein the repayment terms of the Note that is secured by the mortgage are modified in favor of the borrower to make repayment less burdensome. There are several variables in play here. It is critically important for you to understand the range of possible outcomes and the likelihood of attaining the desired outcome. Will the lender lower my interest rate? Will the lender reduce the principal balance on the loan so that it is consistent with the lesser fair market value of the property? Will the lender forego the payments I have missed and add them onto the back end of the loan? Will the lender extend the mortgage term from the original term? These are all possible outcomes when you seek a loan modification. The key lies in understanding the probability of attaining the specific outcomes.

For starters, you need to know a couple key things. First, there is no magic loan modifier out there. There is no person, company, or guru that exists that can deliver all of these outcomes. The reason is that no loan can be modified unless the lender consents. It is therefore the position of the lender with respect to your particular loan situation that will ultimately control the range of outcomes. The second key is that, throughout the entire Financial Crisis, lenders have been extremely reluctant to reduce the principal balance on the note without regard to the degree that the property's market value is less than the mortgage balance. This is an unfortunate situation. In fact, a key campaign position taken by President Obama during his first campaign for the Presidency was that he favored allowing bankruptcy judges to have the power to "cramdown" the balance of a first mortgage on residential property down to the fair market value of the property in a Chapter 13 bankruptcy case. In speech after speech, the President remarked on how appropriate it was for a bankruptcy judge to have this power and pledged his support to change this law.

Sadly, after the election, in the midst of the meltdown of Lehman Brothers, Citicorp, Merrill Lynch, the auto industry and the banking system, all of the economic stimulus initiatives and legislation did not include the bankruptcy cramdown provision. The effort made its way through the House of Representatives with the passage of the Homeowners Relief Act of 2009 – but the bill, which included the cramdown provision sponsored by Senator Chris Dodd of Connecticut, was defeated by a vote in the Senate on April 30, 2009. The defeat was disappointing to those of us who recognized that critical to overcoming the financial hardships caused by the Financial Crisis is creating a valve, where, when appropriate, a homeowner can retain ownership of the home but reduce the mortgage lien on the home so that it is consistent with the FMV of the home. More troubling to me, however, was the way in which the bill went down to defeat. Simply stated, for reasons unknown to me, the Obama Administration apparently abandoned its support of the bill by going "silent" during the critical two weeks during which the bill was a hot topic in committees and on the Senate floor. In Washington, silence is "death" and that's precisely what happened to the Cramdown legislation.

Many people do not realize is that the key to the Cramdown legislation was not its use in actual bankruptcy proceedings. Rather, the greater good from this bill was that it would have created leverage for homeowners to negotiate with lenders outside of bankruptcy because the homeowner, when speaking through their attorney, could remind the lender that if it did not agree to reduce principal as part of the loan modification, the homeowner would seek the assistance of the bankruptcy judge with his "cramdown" authority. In this situation, the anticipation was that the lender would prefer to avoid the cost of the bankruptcy process as well as the potential write-down of the principal balance to current FMV and therefore agree to a compromise by reducing the principal balance so that it was more in line with FMV. The "Cramdown" was thus a leverage tool that could be used in negotiations with the lender in an effort to gain greater concessions, inclusive of principal reductions on the mortgage when the mortgage balance greatly exceeds the market value of the home. The banking industry clearly understood the impact of this legislation outside the bankruptcy process and it's no surprise that intense objections to the bill and lobbying to kill the bill were advanced by the industry. Unfortunately, the banking industry won. I hope and suspect – you're not surprised.

So should you take anything away from this short history on the failed Cramdown legislation? The answer is "yes." Leverage is always the key in any negotiation where two parties are attempting to enter into an agreement or restructure an existing agreement. A loan modification is a restructuring of the loan terms between the lender and the borrower. Though we don't have the "Cramdown tool" to negotiate with the lender, we do have other points that can be made to bolster the argument and persuade the lender that it is in *their interest* to modify the loan on terms that are acceptable to both sides. The one that is most apparent and persuasive to the lender is the risk and costs that attach to foreclosure of the house. The lender understands that unless a modification is reached, the homeowner will allow the house to proceed to foreclosure. When that occurs, the lender knows that the best it can hope for is to recover the property in approximately 9 – 18 months, and that it will have to bear the costs of repairs to the house to ready it for resale, incur selling costs of the property and holding costs until sold. The lender ultimately sells the house for FMV or less in a depressed market and its yield for the liquidation of its security is the proceeds of the sale, less all of these costs that it incurred. Though the lender knows this, if you're negotiating a loan modification, there is no reason not to emphasize these points to the lender.

Practically speaking, the only credible way to make sure the lender understands that its alternative is foreclosure (and it should therefore agree to modify the mortgage) is to seek the modification while behind on your payments. At a minimum, you need to stay at least 59 days behind on your payments, but the better strategy is to withhold all payments on the mortgage so that it appears to the lender that foreclosure is the outcome if there is no modification. Here is where I employ back up plans as part of a modification strategy. Once you are 60 days in arrears on your mortgage, the lender will typically declare the loan to be in "default" and accelerate the entire balance due on the loan in anticipation of commencing foreclosure proceedings. In all states, the process to commence foreclosure, whether by advertisement or judicial sale involves a gap in time before the property actually goes to sale. In virtually all situations, the homeowner has a right to "reinstate" the loan prior to the foreclosure sale by remitting payment of all payments in arrears, late fees and the lender's reasonable costs and attorney fees. It is here that the "backup plan" exists. Suppose your financial crisis management strategy is to obtain a loan modification only and you absolutely do not want to risk losing the home through foreclosure or being in a position where you could be sued on a deficiency? (Keep in mind, every person's situation is different so the first step in the process is to identify what goal you are trying to accomplish. This example assumes the only goal is to modify the mortgage). In this scenario, you can seek the modification while only 59 days in arrears – but the payment history gives an indication to the lender that you may not be willing to allow the house to go to foreclosure and this fact acts as a disincentive to the lender to modify. On the other hand, if you stop making the payments and allow the process to move forward in the foreclosure process, the lender understands that it is looking at having another foreclosed property on its books unless it modifies your mortgage. This is where I want you to be. The "back up plan" is to make sure you save the money from the payments you are not making so that you have it available to reinstate the loan prior to the foreclosure sale in case the modification is not successful.

Of course, this "backup plan" only works in the case where you have the resources to make the mortgage payment and are withholding the payment in an effort to reduce the payment and perhaps gain principal reduction as part of the plan. If you are without the resources to make the payment, your plan and your "back up plan" will, by necessity, be different.

I'm sure you've heard about what seems like a zillion different loan modification programs that the Federal Government and some of the states have adopted in order to streamline the availability of loan modifications for distressed homeowners. In fact, there are several programs and each week new ones are announced and existing ones are modified and changed. To attempt to define them in specific terms in this book would be fruitless because the terms and programs change too rapidly and specific guidelines would be meaningless by the time this book goes to print. There are, however, some basic parameters that you should know that provide a road map to the process.

There are two key Federal Programs that provide the genesis for loan modifications in the marketplace. The largest program is the Home Affordable Modification Program, called the "HAMP" in loan modification circles. This program technically applies to mortgages that are not owned or guaranteed by Fannie Mae or Freddie Mac – the two federally supported agencies that as of mid-2010 owned or guaranteed 53% of the nation's $10.7 trillion in residential mortgages.

Government-Sponsored Enterprise mortgages ("GSEs") are those owned or guaranteed by Fannie Mae, Freddie Mac and FHA, and the GSEs also have their own versions of the HAMP Program and the analysis as to eligibility and procedures are similar and not worthy of distinguishing for purposes of understanding the process.

The other major program that has received positive press and acceptance in the marketplace is the Home Affordable Refinance Program, called "HARP." HARP was initiated in 2009 and for the most part offered no assistance until 2012, when in April, the Obama Administration revised the program. The revision now permits refinancing of first mortgages on all GSE loans owned or guaranteed by Fannie Mae or Freddie Mac without regard to how underwater the homeowner is - so long as they are current on their mortgage obligation. HARP is helpful to those people who are underwater on their home and desire to retain the home and at least gain the benefit of record low mortgage rates in the industry. HARP's greatest benefit is for the homeowner who is only slightly underwater on their house and can benefit by getting rid of a 6% to 8% mortgage and replacing it with the current 3.5% rates that are available.

Almost all major mortgage lenders and loan servicers are participating in the HAMP Program. In order to participate, the servicer must sign a Servicer Participation Agreement. As a condition of participating, the servicer is required to consider all "eligible" mortgage loans for modification. So let's take a look at how HAMP works in order that you can determine if a loan modification under this program falls within the range of options for your consideration. The most critical factor to determine is whether you meet the "eligibility requirements." If you meet the "eligibility requirement," then the next test is whether there is a "positive" or "negative" Net Present Value ("NPV"). If the NPV is "positive" a loan modification must be offered. If it is "negative," it is within the discretion of the servicer to offer a loan modification but it is not mandatory. Even then, if you meet the Eligibility Requirement and the NPV is negative, then HAMP provides other foreclosure alternatives for borrowers under its Home Affordable Foreclosure Alternatives program ("HAFA"). Under HAFA, borrowers who are "eligible" but denied a modification due to the NPV, are afforded greater options to short sell the house or negotiate a deed in lieu in a manner to avoid foreclosure and exposure to deficiency claims.

To be "eligible" under HAMP, the mortgage in question must be a first mortgage given on the property before January 1, 2009. The borrower also cannot have had a previous HAMP modification in connection with the same mortgage. The loan must be delinquent or default must be reasonably foreseeable. If foreclosure proceedings have been commenced, then the default requirement is met and foreclosure does not exclude eligibility. The property must be occupied and the borrower must submit a "Hardship Affidavit." The maximum amount of the unpaid principal balance on the mortgage covering a single unit is $729,750.

So far, these are relatively easy and inconsequential eligibility requirements. The really big one is next. Your Monthly Mortgage Payment Ratio ("MMP Ratio") must be greater than 31%. What does this mean? The ratio is your monthly mortgage payment divided by your Gross Monthly Income, multiplied by 100. For example, if your Gross Monthly Income is $10,000 and your Monthly Mortgage Payment is $3,300, then your MMP Ratio is 33% and you are eligible. (3,300/10,000 = .33 x 100 = 33%). By contrast, if your Monthly Gross Income was $10,000 and your Monthly Mortgage Payment is only $2,800, your MMP Ratio is 28% and you are *not* eligible.   Stated in simpler terms – all you need to do is take your Gross Monthly Income and multiply it by 31%. If that *amount is less than your Monthly Mortgage Payment,* which includes principal, interest, taxes, insurance and condominium association dues (if applicable) then you meet the ratio requirement.

Keep in mind, the Monthly Mortgage Payment includes the monthly interest and principal payment on the first mortgage, plus taxes and insurance, as well as condominium association dues. If taxes, insurance or condo dues are not paid with the mortgage payment then they must be annualized and converted to monthly payments and included in the payment amount. Monthly payments on HELOC, other second and junior liens are *not* included. "Gross Income" refers to your income before deductions for employee paid benefits, taxes, etc. If self-employed, there are criteria established to determine the Gross Monthly Income, but it is basically the net monthly profit from your self-employed business that is considered to be your Gross Monthly Income.

The "Hardship Affidavit" does not impose a problem. The borrower is required to sign an affidavit attesting that they have undergone one or more of the following types of hardship: loss of income, change in household financial circumstances, a recent or upcoming increase in monthly mortgage expense, an increase in other expenses, a lack of sufficient cash reserves to maintain mortgage and living expenses (less than 3 months of covered expenses in savings excluding retirement accounts), excessive monthly debt payments or "other reasons" for hardship. The only other requirement is that if you are "eligible" you must execute a Trial Period Plan by December 31, 2012.

As of this printing, it is undetermined whether HAMP will be extended beyond the current December 31, 2012 expiration date. With the focus of the country being on the upcoming presidential election, it is a "pig and a poke" as to what will happen at the close of the year. Given that the housing industry continues to be the biggest drag on our economy, I am betting that both the HAMP expiration date and the extension of the exclusion from income of cancelation of indebtedness on your principal residence (discussed later) will be extended. Time will tell!

Once "eligibility" has been confirmed, the next critical test is whether the NPV (Net Present Value) is "positive" or "negative." If it is "positive" the servicer *must* offer the loan modification. The NPV test is a software programmed test devised by the Treasury Department that compares the value of the mortgage to the investor with the mortgage modified - compared to the value if not modified. Major servicers are permitted to use their own NPV programs. In essence, the program determines the present value today of the stream of mortgage payments anticipated if the loan is modified compared to the net dollars the investor will yield assuming the property is ultimately sold through the foreclosure process. A "positive" NPV means the value is greater if the loan is modified compared to allowing the property to go through the foreclosure process. Even if the NPV is "negative" the servicer has the discretion under the program to offer a modification.

If the NPV is "positive" the loan modification must be offered. At this point, we need to know what the terms of the modification will be. Here, there is actually a four step process. Step one allows the servicer to capitalize certain expenses and isn't really a concern to us. Step two requires the servicer to reduce the interest rate in increments of 1/8 % (.125) to get the "Target Monthly Mortgage Payment Ratio" to 31%. The floor or maximum that the servicer is required to reduce the interest rate is 2%. If the interest rate reduction does not get the payment ratio to 31%, the next step requires that the term of the mortgage be extended up to 480 months (with interest and payments re-amortized to the new term). If this doesn't get you to the 31% payment ratio, then the servicer must forebear on the principal of the loan to the extent necessary to reach the ratio. Forbearance of principal means that a portion of the principal is tacked on as a balloon at the end of the term (or when the property is sold) and no interest accrues on the balance. Forbearance, unfortunately, is *not the same as principal reduction.* Forbearance does not forgive the amount and it remains an obligation and lien against the property – therefore precluding (or forestalling for a long time) the point in time where you regain equity in the property.

There is an additional step in the process. The servicer is also required to verify the Monthly Gross Expenses of the Borrower. The servicer is required to verify the expense information by running a credit report on the borrower and calculating expenses. The servicer is responsible to determine the "Borrower's Total Monthly Debt Ratio" (also called the "back-end ratio"). I know what you're thinking - not another ratio! Don't shoot the messenger. This ratio is the Total Monthly Expenses divided by Gross Monthly Income, multiplied by 100 to state as a percentage. If the ratio is greater than 55%, the servicer is required to send the Borrower a "Home Affordable Modification Program Counseling Letter." The Borrower is then required to work with a HUD approved counselor on a plan to reduce the debt to less than 55%.

A few observations are in order here. First – the entire analysis of whether you qualify for a HAMP loan modification is *not* dependent on your other monthly expenses. The key is whether your Monthly Mortgage Payment is greater than 31% of your Gross Monthly Income. If it is, as long as the NPV is positive (which it typically is) then you are eligible for a loan modification. The other monthly expense obligations do come into play in the NPV calculation because the model makes an assessment on the likelihood of default if the loan is modified. In this instance, too high a debt burden can impact the NPV determination. Planning is therefore an issue of measuring (and sometimes planning) your Gross Monthly Income. There are circumstances where it may be beneficial to postpone increased income in the period preceding an attempted loan modification in order to meet the 31% eligibility requirement.

Naturally, if you've experienced a material loss of income, as is the case for far too many people, then meeting the eligibility requirement will not be difficult. On the expense side, it is important to examine how expenses are reflected so that, while being realistic, the combination of your other monthly obligations do not adversely cause the risk of default to shift the NPV to negative when NPV is calculated.

Let's run through a quick example to put this in perspective. Let's take the situation for Randy and Beth. Let's assume a monthly mortgage payment of $3,500. Monthly Gross Income, due to the job loss of one spouse has gone from $14,000 to $8,000 (Beth lost her job as a manager of a national boutique chain that closed operations). Let's assume the principal balance on the mortgage is $475,000 and the interest rate is at 7% fixed. The original loan was for $490,000, with a principal and interest payment of $3,260 and taxes and insurance total an additional $749 per month for a total Monthly Mortgage Payment (principal, interest, taxes and insurance) of $4,009. Randy and Beth's Gross Monthly Income before Beth lost her job was $14,000, which when multiplied by 31% equaled $4,340, which is greater than the current payment of $4,009 indicating they would not be eligible. After Beth's job loss, however, their Gross Monthly Income is $8,000, which multiplied by 31% equals $2,480, which is lower than the $4,009 current payment meaning they are now eligible. Let's assume property values in the area are depressed and the NPV is clearly positive. Here's how the modification will play out:

- The new monthly mortgage payment will be $2,480. Of this amount, $1,731.00 will be principal and interest and $749.00 will be for the escrow to cover taxes and insurance.

- The principal balance amortized with interest at 2% per annum with a monthly payment of principal and interest of $1,731.00 is $475,000, payable over 367 months. The 2% rate is applied only for the first two to five years and then scales up to market rate in incremental increases (but capping typically at 3.5% to 4.0%).

In this case, Randy and Beth benefit by the reduction of the monthly mortgage payment from $4,009 to $2,480.

Is a Loan Modification Beneficial?

If you think about it, this is quite a remarkable program and in some respects many homeowners could benefit – but what precisely is the benefit? In the case of a home that is not underwater or is only slightly underwater, the benefit is the homeowner gains a reduction in interest, recapitalization of the payments and taxes in arrears and an potentially an extended term. For the homeowner who is significantly underwater, however, the benefit is marginal without principal reduction. What good is it to retain a home that you owe $475,000 if it is only worth $250,000 even if you have a lower payment? The answer is – very little. The one benefit I do see is that if the lower payment is at a level cheaper than the rental market, you gain the benefit of retaining the home and the right to live there at a monthly cost that is less than rent. Additionally, under present tax laws you retain the interest and real property tax itemized deduction as well.

On the flip side, however, you remain stuck in a home that has no short or even medium term potential to be an asset – such as one that you can pledge to a bank to support an equity loan to use to start a business or make an investment. I believe this is the crux of our nation's biggest problem in regenerating our economy. The analysis is rather simple and builds on key "economic facts" we so often hear:

- Consumer spending is the largest factor that drives our economy. Consumers must be employed to drive spending.

- Job creation by small business is the key to increasing employment, which, in turn, increases consumer spending.

- Small businesses must be able to obtain small business loans from commercial lenders to start businesses.

- Commercial lenders do not make "unsecured" loans and have typically looked to second mortgages against personal residences as the collateral to support new start up business loans.

- There is presently no equity cushion in personal residences (or the vast amount of commercial property) in the U.S. as a result of the Financial Crisis and thus there is no collateral to support making loans.

The HAMP modification program, as well as the lender based programs that modify without principal reduction, do nothing to address the "equity cushion" problem. Other than the "cheaper than rent" outcome, these programs do not provide a mechanism to shed the underwater house that is toxic to your economic health. Under HAMP, unless your monthly mortgage payment exceeds your monthly gross income by 31%, and in reality, a significant margin beyond 32%, you will not even realize the "cheaper than rent" benefit. This means the genesis of the help the Government is providing is to assist those homeowners who have sustained a significant income drop. The only other class that meets the eligibility criteria is a homeowner, who acquired a home with a mortgage that was disproportionately too expensive for their income. The vast majority of underwater homeowners, however, do not fit within this class. Keep in mind, as of May, 2012, sixteen million Americans are underwater in their homes and the average price of homes has fallen 35% from 2008.

The purpose of reviewing the tools for Financial Crisis Management is to determine which tools have functional utility in specific circumstances. In this context, it is important to understand that a loan modification will not assist the homeowner whose critical loss in this crisis is the decline in market value of the home. This homeowner, who has income, will not benefit from a loan modification and if he takes no action, he will use his future income to cover the market decline in the home rather than to secure his future retirement.

In this context, it is important to understand that a loan modification will not assist the homeowner whose critical loss in this crisis is the decline in market value of the home. This homeowner, who has income, will not benefit from a loan modification and if he takes no action, he will use his future income to cover the market decline in the home rather than to secure his future retirement.

So what about Principal Reduction?

Until recently, there has been a lot of talk and little action in getting lenders to agree to include principal reduction in loan modifications. One of the largest impediments has been the refusal of Ed DeMarco, the head of the Federal Housing Finance Agency ("FHFA") which provides oversight of Fannie Mae and Freddie Mac to endorse the concept. The main policy reason cited by Mr. Demarco and the mortgage industry is that permitting principal reduction on mortgages would lead to massive numbers of individuals seeking "strategic defaults" to take advantage of the program. I fume over this issue. Financial crisis management certainly endorses and encourages the notion of a strategic default in order to exit a house underwater. The choice is to short sell the property or modify the mortgage with a reduction in the principal balance on the mortgage note. Is this wrong or a terrible thing? If you accept the premise that our economy is built on the notion of the growth of small business and that banks will not provide the lending needed to facilitate small business start-ups without collateral in the form of second mortgages on houses with equity – then you need to do something! The solution is that the strategic default is not a pandemic that needs to be avoided – it is the solution to our housing problem and overall economic problem. Allowing principal reduction would simply resolve the problem quicker by giving people an alternative to short selling the property or employing other tools of Financial Crisis Management to exit the house underwater.

The solution is that the strategic default is not a pandemic that needs to be avoided – it is the solution to our housing problem and overall economic problem.

Principal reduction – though not readily available, is possible in some modification situations. Under the National Mortgage Settlement that was finalized in April, 2012 (go to www.nationalmortgagesettlement.com for details), the five major lenders, Bank of America, JPMorgan Chase, Wells Fargo, GMAC/Ally, and Citi are all bound to provide significant principal reduction on mortgage obligations as a means of satisfying the vast majority of the $25 Billion dollar settlement. The mechanics as to which borrowers are to be offered principal reduction are not presently known and it appears that the lenders are able to make the determination internally without disclosing criteria or permitting any formal application process so long as they are able to substantiate compliance under the terms of the settlement. Additionally, other lenders have demonstrated some willingness to include some principal reduction in approved loan modifications. The important point here from a financial crisis management perspective is that if principal reduction would be a good fit with the overall plan of action, consideration should be given to attempting a modification effort in advance of short selling or other options assuming such a course can be accommodated in the plan.

Loan Modifications – A Sneaky Purpose

Loan Modifications, as a tool in Financial Crisis Management, also have a collateral, somewhat sneaky, function. In circumstances where the financial crisis strategy has been determined to require the shedding of the excessive mortgage debt by allowing the home to proceed through foreclosure, the strategic plan is to allow the homeowner to remain in possession of the home as long as possible in order to allow the homeowner to save money by sparing them the monthly mortgage payment. In this scenario, it is in the homeowner's interest to allow the process to go as slowly as possible. The process of loan modification takes time. Lenders now typically suspend the foreclosure process while the loan modification process is being pursued in earnest by the homeowner. Thus, it can be beneficial to start and complete the loan modification process as a means of delaying the ultimate commencement of foreclosure proceedings. Remember, the goal is to attain your objectives. The lender, of course, will wince at the thought of such a strategy, but we'll leave the sympathies and such matters for their industry to fess over.

7

The Bankruptcy Laws

Bankruptcy is a tool of Financial Crisis Management. As a tool, we use it in two ways. On a frequent basis, we remind the creditors we deal with that we are bankruptcy attorneys, representing our clients for Financial Crisis Management and that if matters cannot be resolved on a satisfactory basis, we will file for bankruptcy relief. This is using the "threat of bankruptcy" as a tool to persuade the particular creditor to reach terms that we find to be acceptable and consistent with the plan. The "threat of bankruptcy" is critical to negotiations we pursue with junior mortgage holders and the credit card industry in Debt Resolution. The threat doesn't really have significant impact with the first mortgage holders because they are secured by the first lien on the property. The distinction is that the first mortgage holder has a secured claim so the vast majority of its protection is derived from the property as the security. The junior mortgage holders, whose liens do not attach to any equity due to the depressed values of real estate, as well as the credit card companies, hold what we call "unsecured claims." In bankruptcy proceedings, unsecured creditors are used to receiving nothing for their claims. Because of this, the threat of bankruptcy to an unsecured creditor carries greater magnitude and if they believe the threat to be genuine they are apt to settle their claim for small dollars.

Beyond the "threat of bankruptcy," the actual filing of bankruptcy proceedings is a valued tool in Financial Crisis Management. There are three basic types of bankruptcy cases for individuals. They are named by the chapters they reside in the Bankruptcy Code. For our purposes, you need to understand which chapters we use to accomplish the appropriate tasks in the context of financial crisis management and realizing our ultimate goal of shedding debt and preserving future income. In this context, the optimal case is a Chapter 7 Bankruptcy. In this type of case, an individual is able to discharge all of his debts existing as of the date the bankruptcy case is filed, excluding certain nondischargeable claims such as certain tax and divorce obligations, student loans, as well as debts procured by fraud and other improper actions that are not germane for this discussion. The other major type of case filed for individuals is a Chapter 13 Bankruptcy which is often called a wage-earners plan or debt adjustment for individuals. Chapter 13 applies only to "individuals with regular income" and is akin to what I call a personal reorganization where debts are adjusted downward and extension on the time frame to pay is achieved. Chapter 13's greatest feature from a financial crisis management perspective is that it's the ideal type of case to file in order to stop a foreclosure of the house and seek to cure all mortgage payments that have been missed. As will be explained shortly, Chapter 13 has limitations as to the amount of unsecured and secured debt a person is allowed. Chapter 11, which is the formal "reorganization" chapter for businesses, as well as individuals, is available in situations where the individual does not meet the Chapter 13 debt limitations.

Chapter 7 is often referred to as the "fresh start" case. To file a Chapter 7 case, the individual's attorney prepares a bankruptcy petition. The petition lists the assets the person owns, along with his or her secured and unsecured claims to all creditors. A limited number of exemptions is allowed on the asset side, including, but not limited to, a $21,625 Homestead exemption, up to $3,450 equity in a motor vehicle and a wildcard exemption. The person filing the case is referred to as the "debtor." Under the laws of some states, the debtor has a choice between the specified federal exemptions or those provided under the laws of the debtor's state, and in other states the state exemptions apply to the exclusion of the federal exemptions. When a Chapter 7 case is completed, the debtor obtains a "discharge" of his or her pre-petition debts with the benefit of not having to pay any of the debt on a going forward basis. Though certain debts such as student loans, child support, alimony and divorce property settlements are not dischargeable, the vast majority of pre-petition debt is dischargeable. Obtaining the discharge combined with the retention of the specified exempt property is the operable event in providing the person a "fresh start."

Given my view that the goal of Financial Crisis Management is to preserve future income and to avoid allowing it to be used to pay debts of the past, a Chapter 7 case, when applicable, can be an ideal tool. Chapter 7, however, is not the tool we use when seeking to save a house from foreclosure and unfortunately, with the revisions to the Bankruptcy Code in 2005, Chapter 7, when desired, is not always available.

The availability of Chapter 7 relief for individuals was limited by The Bankruptcy Abuse Prevention and Consumer Protection Act of 2005 (called "BABCPA") as a result of intensive and successful lobbying efforts of the banking industry. The 2005 amendments changed over 100 years of bankruptcy law. The most critical change in the law is that the amendments created what is referred to as "Means Testing," which has the effect of precluding someone from filing a

Chapter 7 case in circumstances where they have regular income. The regular income creates the "means" to pay back a portion of the debt. If you have such regular income, you "fail" the Means Test and if you do not meet any other available exception allowing for Chapter 7, you are precluded from filing a Chapter 7 case and obtaining the discharge. In this situation you must file a Chapter 13 case if you qualify, and if not, a Chapter 11 reorganization.

Chapter 7 Eligibility

An individual files his or her case in the federal district where he or she has resided the most during the 180 days immediately preceding the filing of the case. If you have previously obtained a Chapter 7 discharge, you must wait eight years after the last filing of a Chapter 7 case to file another. The prime goal in filing a Chapter 7 case is to obtain a fresh start. In this context, "the debtor is exchanging his or her nonexempt property for the forgiveness of dischargeable debts." This quoted sentence speaks to two key issues. You are only able to retain "exempt property" which means the non-exempt property will be subject to sale by the trustee in order to liquidate the asset and provide funds to distribute to the creditors. Secondly, the discharge does not apply to "nondischargeable debts."

The exempt property is the property which the individual is allowed to retain when filing a Chapter 7 case. Depending upon the state in which you are filing the case, you are permitted to either elect the federal exemptions or the state law exemptions or you must use the state exemptions. This can be a sensitive issue that calls for the expertise of the bankruptcy attorney to address. The goal is to select the exemption scheme that will protect your most valued assets. The Federal Exemptions are listed in 11 USC 522 (you can readily find this on the Internet using a search engine). The primary federal exemptions are:

Property	Federal Exemption Values as of April 1, 2010
Household–one item	$ 550
Household Items – aggregate (no single item > $550)	11,525
Motor Vehicle	3,450
Tools of the Trade	2,175
Homestead	21,625
Wildcard	10,825* + 1,150
Jewelry	1,450
Life Insurance	11,525
	* Only available to the extent the homestead exemption is not used and limited to ½ the amount

The Wildcard, in the aggregate totals, $11,975 when the debtor is not utilizing any of the Homestead exemption. This exemption is typically used to protect cash. The exemptions are per debtor, so if a husband and wife are filing, together they are each entitled to the various exemptions. There are a total of 21 types of debts listed under 11 USC 523(a) of the Bankruptcy Code that are nondischargeable. This list includes marital debts and support obligations, taxes (some of which are dischargeable), student loans, debts procured through fraud, as well as fraudulent conveyances.

The critical path to eligibility for obtaining a discharge in a Chapter 7 case is whether you will need to pass the Means Test, and if so, whether you do in fact pass the test. If your debts are not primarily consumer debts then you are not subject to the Means Test calculation. Consumer debts are debts incurred by an individual primarily for a personal, family or household purpose. A mortgage debt on your residence or vacation property is consumer debt. Credit card debt can be consumer or non-consumer debt depending upon the nature of the purchases made. Debts arising from personal guarantees of business debts are non-consumer debts. Income tax liabilities and student loans have been determined to be consumer debts.

We call this the Business Debt vs. Consumer Debt analysis when I review a client's situation. In many cases, clients in financial crisis have substantial business debt due to a business failure. The business failure, coupled with adverse real estate holdings, has placed the client in crisis. This same client may still have solid income from his profession or other businesses which, as we will discuss shortly, makes a Chapter 7 unavailable if the client is subject to the Means Test calculation. Suppose, however, you have significant debts arising from guarantees on a failed business venture, along with significant credit card debt some of which is consumer and some of which is business. Additionally, suppose you are substantially underwater on your house along with rental properties that no longer have tenants. In this situation, we carefully analyze the business debt compared to the consumer debt and look for strategies where we can derive an outcome where your business debt exceeds your consumer debt. If we can accomplish this task, then (subject to some abuse limitations in certain jurisdictions) you will be eligible to file a Chapter 7 case and discharge the debts rather than being forced into either a Chapter 13 or Chapter 11 case.

There are two major strategies that we've used. Typically, the greatest chance to shift the ratio of business versus consumer debt is to eliminate consumer mortgage debt. This can be achieved by allowing the house to go through foreclosure or elimination of the debt through a deed in lieu of foreclosure or short sale. Once the mortgage debt is discharged or to the extent it is discharged, the ratio of business debt will increase compared to consumer debt. In situations where we've been able to narrow the margin, we've then settled out on some of the consumer credit card debt by settling those claims for 10-20 cents on the dollar in order to shift the balance so that post settlement, the business debt exceeds the consumer debt. Once this is accomplished, we can file the Chapter 7 case and discharge all dischargeable debt without regard to the income of the client. Such a result can preserve thousands and thousands of future income!

Beyond the Business Debt vs. Consumer Debt rule to avoid the Means Test in a Chapter 7, disabled veterans whose debt was primarily incurred when on active duty or while performing defense activity in the homeland are not subject to the Means Test calculation.

The Means Test Calculation

There is a two-step process in passing the Means Test. Remember, if you pass the "Means Test" you are eligible to seek the discharge in Chapter 7. If you fail the "Means Test" you must file under Chapter 13 if eligible, and if not, then under Chapter 11 if you want to gain benefits under the bankruptcy laws. In this sense, the term "Means Test," in my view, is reversed. It is easier for me to understand the notion that if I have the "means" to pay back some of my debt; I should not be eligible for a Chapter 7 case. Thus, what the rule is saying is that "if you have the means to pay back some of your debt, you fail the Means Test and you cannot file a Chapter 7." I hope this helps clarify the issue. You can typically count on one thing in the law, if there is a more confusing way to say something then that will be the approach taken!

The first component requires an analysis of the person's current monthly income which is referred to as their CMI. This is the average monthly income from all sources that the debtor receives in the preceding six-month period ending on the last day of the calendar month preceding the date the case is filed. CMI is broadly defined and includes the income of both spouses even if only one spouse is filing (unless, in limited circumstances it can be proven that the non-filing spouse keeps his or her finances separate). Once the six month average CMI is calculated, it is multiplied by 12 and compared to the applicable state's annual medium income for the same size household according to the U.S. Census Bureau. If your CMI is less than the average, there is no presumption of abuse and you will be able to proceed with a Chapter 7 without any further means testing. The effect of CMI is that the higher the CMI, the greater chance exists that you will not pass the first component of the test leaving you in the situation where you have to continue to the second step of the process.

Here is the Census Bureau Median Income by Family Size:

Census Bureau Median Family Income by Family Size (Cases Filed On and After May 1, 2012)			
State	**Family Size** (*Add $7,500 for each individual in excess of 4)		
	1 Person	**2 People**	**3 People**	**4 People ***
	$39,531	$47,478	$52,798	$63,537
Alaska	$54,272	$73,046	$79,637	$90,781
Arizona	$42,691	$55,479	$58,292	$63,201
Arkansas	$35,283	$45,438	$48,520	$58,051
California	$49,188	$63,481	$68,135	$77,167
Colorado	$48,856	$64,402	$71,438	$82,427
Connecticut	$58,565	$72,562	$82,797	$102,579
Delaware	$49,566	$61,819	$73,508	$82,349
District of Columbia	$52,148	$80,785	$80,785	$119,656
Florida	$42,053	$51,299	$54,508	$64,722
Georgia	$40,947	$52,313	$57,470	$66,250
Hawaii	$52,712	$64,403	$78,296	$85,337
Idaho	$40,355	$50,796	$53,721	$63,236
Illinois	$46,983	$59,794	$68,865	$81,570
Indiana	$41,249	$51,237	$59,517	$69,420

Iowa	$41,933	$56,960	$64,216	$74,514
Kansas	$42,924	$57,562	$64,834	$74,959
Kentucky	$39,567	$46,107	$53,496	$64,558
Louisiana	$39,128	$47,626	$56,363	$67,854
Maine	$41,811	$53,371	$62,095	$77,097
Maryland	$59,269	$76,281	$86,807	$104,114
Massachusetts	$55,185	$66,200	$82,873	$102,194
Michigan	$45,056	$51,660	$60,313	$72,454
Minnesota	$47,618	$63,101	$74,050	$86,910
Mississippi	$34,172	$42,914	$46,973	$56,494
Missouri	$40,123	$52,200	$60,197	$69,378
Montana	$39,580	$51,313	$58,085	$70,469
Nebraska	$40,429	$57,271	$66,742	$73,496
Nevada	$44,508	$57,327	$62,776	$67,236
New Hampshire	$53,177	$63,626	$81,854	$94,646
New Jersey	$62,226	$69,634	$87,576	$105,175
New Mexico	$38,422	$51,078	$53,417	$56,365
New York	$47,381	$57,884	$69,066	$83,775
North Carolina	$39,088	$50,248	$56,024	$67,089
North Dakota	$44,309	$60,596	$69,367	$81,840
Ohio	$41,748	$51,839	$60,219	$72,827
Oklahoma	$38,649	$49,838	$55,015	$62,301
Oregon	$44,230	$53,967	$59,242	$68,719
Pennsylvania	$46,515	$54,767	$68,586	$79,102
Rhode Island	$47,798	$61,506	$68,909	$88,990
South Carolina	$38,849	$49,363	$52,428	$64,898
South Dakota	$37,961	$56,763	$63,557	$71,184
Tennessee	$39,165	$48,725	$53,272	$62,832
Texas	$40,925	$55,653	$59,650	$65,875
Utah	$49,697	$57,309	$61,508	$66,825
Vermont	$44,918	$56,850	$71,937	$79,736
Virginia	$52,202	$66,317	$73,905	$90,260
Washington	$53,302	$63,873	$71,379	$82,942
West Virginia	$42,178	$45,407	$52,596	$63,638
Wisconsin	$43,202	$57,428	$66,767	$78,520
Wyoming	$50,373	$64,031	$69,176	$75,678

Needless to say, the lower the CMI, the greater ease it is to qualify for a Chapter 7 filing. An interesting component in determining CMI is the effect that drawing money from an IRA or 401(k) has on the calculation of CMI. The present law in this area is not clear. Some jurisdictions include withdrawals from a person's IRA or 401(k) in the calculation of CMI. I want to point this out for two important reasons. First, this is an unfair and unfortunate result because these funds represent monies that you've already earned and when you draw them from your retirement, they are not recurring sources of income so they should not be included in the calculation of CMI. Remember, our goal is to keep CMI down. The second and much more important point that I want to emphasize is that YOU SHOULD NEVER, NEVER, NEVER borrow from your IRA or 401(k) to pay credit card debt or to service a mortgage on a house underwater. These funds are protected in bankruptcy proceedings and under virtually all state laws so that a creditor cannot get to these funds in or outside of bankruptcy. Taking this money from your retirement and using it to pay past debts, in my view, is like burning it. There are limited exceptions to this rule, but you need to proceed cautiously and only on the advice of an independent professional who has thoroughly analyzed the issue. Since I have never been a fan of fire, I will tell you one more time:

> **NEVER, NEVER, NEVER BORROW FROM YOUR IRA OR 401(K) TO PAY CREDIT CARD DEBT OR TO SERVICE A MORTGAGE ON A HOUSE UNDERWATER UNLESS YOU CONSULT WITH A PROFESSIONAL ADVISOR WHO THOROUGHLY EXAMINED THE ISSUE.**

Let's move on. If your annualized income is greater than the annual medium income, the next phase requires that a determination be made whether your income is sufficient to fund a meaningful repayment plan in a Chapter 13 case. If the answer is yes, then you will have failed the Means Test and you cannot file a Chapter 7 case. If the answer is no, you will have passed the Means Test and absent one more hurdle you will be on your way to a Chapter 7 discharge.

This test is often called the "net disposable income test." The test results works like this. Your bankruptcy attorney will evaluate your expenses to determine your annual expenses to be charged against annual income. Under the Bankruptcy Code, the numbers are evaluated from the standpoint of the total dividend that would be paid to your unsecured creditors over a 60 Month plan. It's easier in some respects to think of this number in terms of Annual Disposable Income or Monthly Disposable Income, which are both determined by dividing the 60 month number by 5 for the annual and by 60 for the monthly. The rules work this way:

Net Disposable Income Test Rules

1. If the net disposable income for the 60 month plan is greater than $11,725 (which is $2,345 annually and $195.41 monthly) then you *can* provide a meaningful repayment plan under Chapter 13 and you FAIL the Means Test.

2. If the net disposable income for the 60 month plan is less than $7,025 (which is $1,405 annually and $117.08 monthly) then you *cannot* provide a meaningful repayment plan under Chapter 13 and you PASS the Means Test.

3. If the net disposable income for the 60 month plan is less than $11,725 ($2,345 annually and $195.41 monthly) and greater than $7,025 ($1,405 annually and $117.08 monthly) AND the 60 month amount is greater than 25% of your unsecured claims then you *can* provide a meaningful repayment plan under Chapter 13 and you FAIL the Means Test.

4.   If the net disposable income for the 60 month plan is less than $11,725 ($2,345 annually and $195.41 monthly) and greater than $7,025 ($1,405 annually and $117.08 monthly) AND the 60 month amount is LESS than or EQUAL to 25% of your unsecured claims then you *cannot* provide a meaningful repayment plan under Chapter 13 and you FAIL the Means Test.

Stated another way, this test says you are eligible for a Chapter 7 case and do not have to proceed under Chapter 13 (or Chapter 11) if: (1) your Monthly Disposable Income is less than $117.08; or (2) if your Monthly Disposable Income is greater than $117.08 but less than $195.41 *and* 25% of your total unsecured claims equals is greater than $11,725 (i.e. your unsecured debt is more than $46,900). These determinations are "presumptions" which means that absent evidence substantiating "special circumstances" the rules are applied as stated.

Evaluation of expenses in the calculation of net disposable income is a process that requires application of limits to specific categories dictated by the process. National standards define the limits on expenses for food, housekeeping, apparel, supplies and services, etc. These limitations are explained in the Internal Revenue Service Manual and can be found on the web at www.irs.gov/irm/part5/irm_05-015-001.html. I guess it's no surprise that the website link is as convoluted as the rest of the federal framework. To give you the flavor of the limitations, the National Standard for "food, housekeeping supplies, apparel and services, personal care products and services, and miscellaneous" are set forth in the following chart:

IRS NATIONAL STANDARDS FOOD, HOUSING, etc. Effective on April 2, 2102				
Expense	**One Person**	**Two Persons**	**Three Persons**	**Four Persons**
Food	$ 301	$ 537	$ 639	$ 765
Housekeeping supplies	30	66	65	74
Apparel & services	86	162	209	244
Personal care products & services	32	55	63	67
Misc.	116	209	251	300
Total	**$ 565**	**$ 1,029**	**$ 1,227**	**$ 1.450**

For each additional person, you add $281 to the four person allowance. The guidelines may be exceeded by up to 5% for food and clothing if the excess is reasonable and necessary.

If the Means Test is passed, absent unusual circumstances, the case can proceed as a Chapter 7. The rest of the process is easy from the individual's perspective. After the case is filed, it is unlawful for any creditor to contact you or take any affirmative action to pursue its claim except through the bankruptcy process. The phone calls stop, the hassle ends. You will need to attend a "meeting of creditors," which is commonly known as a "341 Hearing." The hearing is conducted by the U.S. Trustee assigned to the case and typically occurs 4 to 6 weeks after the case is filed. The hearing is quick, you appear with your counsel, state your name, that you read your petition when you signed it and that it was true then and true now. The trustee and any creditors can attend and ask you questions. In the normal situation, that is the only appearance you make. Approximately 8 to 12 weeks later, a discharge is granted by the court and mailed to you.

Discharge of Taxes

Another often unknown and forgotten benefit of Chapter 7 and a Chapter 13 case is that certain income tax obligations are dischargeable. There are three basic rules, plus two additional ones: (1) The due date for the return has to be at least 3 years prior to the filing of the case; (2) the actual return had to be filed at least 2 years prior to the filing of the case; and (3) the tax had to be assessed at least 240 days prior to the filing of the case. The two additional rules are that the return cannot be fraudulent and the taxpayer cannot be guilty of income tax evasion.

Proper analysis of the dischargeability of income taxes is a critical factor that must be carefully scrutinized before a bankruptcy case is filed. We find many bankruptcy practitioners are remiss on this point because they are not familiar with the process of obtaining a taxpayer's tax transcript from the IRS which correctly provides the necessary information in order to determine whether the necessary time has run to discharge the tax debt. You certainly don't want to find out too late is that had you waited a week or month longer before filing the case, a tax liability would have been discharged - and now you're stuck with it. If you have tax debt and are considering filing bankruptcy – be sure your attorney pulls the IRS transcripts and verifies the status of all unpaid tax liabilities.

Chapter 13

Chapter 13 is often called the "wage-earner's plan" or "debt adjustment plan" and is a trustee supervised reorganization of an individual's debts. In a situation where an individual fails the Means Test, we evaluate whether they can derive a benefit from a Chapter 13 case. There are, however, several circumstances, where a Chapter 13 case, on its own, is a valuable tool in Financial Crisis Management. There are primarily four sets of circumstances where Chapter 13 can provide a positive outcome that is not available through a Chapter 7 filing.

The first and I'd say the foremost compelling reason to file a Chapter 13 case is that it is the only way a homeowner can stop a mortgage lender from pursuing foreclosure of the house and allow for the right to cure the missed payments over the course of the plan. Of course, a loan modification could achieve the same result, but this can only occur on a consensual basis with the lender – which, unfortunately, is often not available. Another key benefit to a Chapter 13 case is that if you have a second, third or other junior mortgage on your residence and there is no equity attaching to the security because the fair market value of the home is less than the first mortgage, then these junior mortgages can be stripped of all secured value and treated as an unsecured claim. Similarly, Chapter 13 allows you to strip the lien of first and all junior mortgage lenders on real estate that is not your personal residence. To the extent the mortgage balances exceed the market value of the real estate; such amounts can be treated as unsecured claims.

Chapter 13 allows you to save a vehicle from repossession or if the vehicle has been repossessed, you can compel the return of the vehicle. Chapter 13 is also a valuable tool in situations where you own real or personal property with significant equity and wish to retain these assets. Keep in mind; under Chapter 7 you only are able to retain the exempt assets. Beyond the exemptions, the remaining assets are property of the bankruptcy estate and it is the Chapter 7 trustee's duty to sell these assets for the benefit of the creditors. Chapter 13, on the other hand, allows you to retain the assets. The tradeoff is that the value of the equity in these assets is taken into account in the determination of the amount that is to be paid to your creditors over the life of the plan.

Qualification Limits in Chapter 13

In order to be eligible to file a Chapter 13 case, the filer must be an individual with regular income and meet the debt limitations. The maximum amount of unsecured debt is $360,475 and the maximum amount of secured debt is $1,081,400. These amounts adjust every three years based upon changes in the Consumer Price Index. The next adjustment date is April 1, 2013.

Chapter 13 Timeline and Process

Once the Chapter 13 case is commenced, the 341 meeting of creditors is scheduled 25 to 45 days later. This hearing serves the same function as in a Chapter 7 case. The only additional hearing for the filer to typically appear in a Chapter 13 case is the Confirmation Hearing. The Chapter 13 case requires that a Chapter 13 Plan be filed. All creditors are provided a copy of the plan, as well as the Chapter 13 trustee who supervises the process. The plan is approved through the confirmation process. During the period between the filing of the proposed plan and the Confirmation Hearing, which is scheduled approximately 90 days following the filing of the case, objections from the trustee and creditors can be filed and the debtor's attorney seeks to resolve these issues in advance of the hearing or, if not resolved, the matters are addressed by the bankruptcy court judge at the Confirmation Hearing.

The Chapter 13 Plan length ranges between 36 and 60 months. The length of the plan is determined by the Means Test. As explained in the discussion of Chapter 7, if the filer's median income is equal to or below the median income for the state and household size, then the plan is 36 to 60 months. If median income is above the median income for the state and household size, the plan must run for 60 months. If creditors are to be paid in full, the plan can be less than the required periods. Keep in mind, if you are below the median income, you "pass" the Means Test and could possibly pursue a Chapter

7 case. This means that the reason the Chapter 13 would be filed in such a situation is to derive one of the benefits available in a Chapter 13 that is not available under Chapter 7.

Once the plan is completed, the process is complete and the court will issue the discharge - which discharges the debtor from any further liability on all dischargeable claims.

How Chapter 13 Can Help

There are times when a Chapter 13 filing can be a valuable tool. Let's suppose you have steady income but you are saddled with credit card debt and underwater in your home due to the second mortgage. Here are the facts:

Monthly Income	-	$ 8,000
FMV – Residence	-	200,000
1st Mortgage	-	205,000
2nd Mortgage	-	60,000
Credit Card Debt	-	100,000

Monthly Disposable Income under the Means Test - $250.00 per month. (This means, the Monthly Budget, which is CMI – less the allowable National and Local Standards yields a positive $250.00 per month).

Given these facts, this individual does not qualify for a Chapter 7 since his monthly disposable income over 60 months will fund a $15,000 plan ($250 x 60 = $15,000). In simple terms, here is what will transpire. The $60,000 second mortgage on the home will become an unsecured claim since there is no equity attaching to it. Total unsecured claims will therefore equal the credit card debt of $100,000, plus the second mortgage of $60,000, for a total of $160,000. The amount available to fund the plan is $15,000. Of this amount, approximately $5,000 will be paid to cover the attorney fees and trustee fees in the case, yielding a payment of $10,000 for the unsecured claims, payable over 60 months to satisfy a total of $160,000 in claims. This amounts to a payout of 9.38% over 60 months without interest. In this case, the family retains the home without the second mortgage and discharges the unsecured debt for far less than through debt resolution or other alternatives.

Chapter 11 Reorganization

Chapter 11, which is the business reorganization provision of the Bankruptcy Code, is also available for individuals. The process is complex and costly. Chapter 11 is nonetheless a tool used in financial crisis management. For individuals, I consider it a tool of last resort due to its cost. At the same time, if your financial situation is such that you need the protection from creditors available through the bankruptcy process but you cannot pass the Means Test due as a result of your income being too high and you fail to meet the debt qualification limits of Chapter 13, then Chapter 11 must be considered as a viable alternative.

8

Debt Resolution

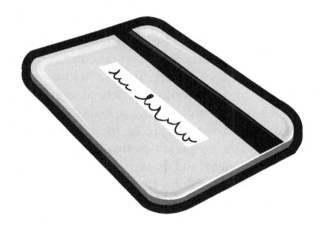

I refer to the process of compromising credit card debt as "Debt Resolution." The Financial Crisis has witnessed an onslaught of "Debt Settlement" companies that seek to assist people in settling out their credit card obligations at a discount. Before addressing some of my misgivings as to the business practices of these Debt Settlement companies, let's explore my approach to Debt Resolution.

First and foremost, you must recognize that the credit card companies will not discount or assist you if you're paying the cards current. The collateral consequence here is that you must stop paying on the cards in order to derive the best discount. This means, if you're overly concerned with your credit score you're going to have a difficult time taking advantage of the terrific results that can be achieved using Debt Resolution as a tool for Financial Crisis Management. Remember Mike and Rita – is it better to have a net worth in 20 years of $29,000 or $840,000? Dumping your debt is the key to this outcome and, in my view, far outweighs the cost of seeing your credit score dip for a couple of years.

Before going too far, let's discuss the basics of when Debt Resolution is a good idea. The best case scenario is someone with substantial credit card debt who still has regular income such that we can facilitate settlement of the card balances by saving the money that was being paid to service the monthly payments on the cards. Even better is the situation where that same person has, for one reason or another, already let his credit slip such that his or her credit score is low – which in my view is a rating of 550 or less. Often times, I employ this strategy on clients who are seeking a loan modification, short sale or deed in lieu of foreclosure on their house ("not home") or other property. The reason is that this is a person who we are attempting to shed debt and preserve future income without utilizing a bankruptcy filing. Keep in mind, while I think bankruptcy is a great solution when you can pass the "Means Test" and discharge debt, the current law does not always cooperate. Fortunately, Debt Resolution can facilitate reaching the designated goal.

A critically important component that must be analyzed before making any decision to use Debt Resolution is whether you will incur tax consequences from settling the debt. When credit card debt is settled, the credit card company always issues an IRS Form 1099-C as to the amount of debt that is forgiven. The forgiveness of debt is taxable as ordinary income unless you meet one of the exceptions which is discussed in detail later under *Tax Issues*. You need to know, up front, if there will be tax consequences or not, and if so, whether it makes sense to use this tool of Financial Crisis Management.

Debt Resolution – The Process

Here's how the process works. Once I decide a client is right for debt resolution, I have them provide me with a copy of each of their credit card statements. I instruct them to stop making payments on the cards effective immediately. The first issue we then encounter is a discussion as to how to handle phone calls received from the credit card companies. In today's market, the day following the due date for a payment, calling begins in earnest by the card issuers seeking payment. My preference in this situation is to have the client take the calls from the credit card companies for a limited period of 30 to 45 days if they have the personal stamina to field all the calls and "take the heat" so to speak.

I tell the client that it is important to talk politely to the card company issuers and explain to them how bad your feel that you are behind but that your income has been cut and you simply don't have any money to pay them. Here's is why. Each time you speak to a representative who is calling you, they are sitting in front of a computer screen and making notes of your call. These notes, over time, build into a history. Down the road, after many calls first to the client and then to my office, we're going to be on the phone with someone attempting to reach a settlement on the claim. When that eventually happens, the decision to accept a settlement always requires the approval of a supervisor in the credit card collection or third party collection department. The supervisor will have never spoken to the client or me as of that date. The supervisor's only method of deciding to accept the settlement or to reject it and hold out for more money is going to be based on his review of the file. So what is the file? The file is that computer screen that lists all relevant data on your account, the pay history and the default history along with all of the comments that have been placed into the file when the collection calls are made.

There are two impressions that I want to make on the supervisor. One – that we have consistently explained the dire financial condition that you are in such that bankruptcy was the only likely option in the near future. This is critical so that the supervisor is of the mindset to take what money he or she can get before it is too late. The second is that the client is a good person and that if there was any way they could have repaid this debt they certainly would have. To support this second point, I try to enlist the client to approach the calls with flair of drama by playing the role of the disheartened victim- always being polite and expressing apologies for not being able to pay. To the women, I tell them an occasional crying spell, if not too dramatic, is a nice touch! Maybe in some ways I'm a bit crazy here – but I find Debt Resolution to be one of the more pleasant aspects of financial crisis management. Taking into account the pressure and despair that my clients are enduring, I try and shift the emotions to make this a challenge for them with a bit of levity. Make no mistake – we're talking acting here – because the goal is to pay them as little as possible. What is equally important here is that the "computer file," when reviewed by the supervisor, does not indicate that the card holder is hostile, angry or threatening. Keep in mind; I understand that hostility is common and many times an appropriate emotion to be experiencing if you are in financial crisis. My point is that conveying such sentiments do not serve our goal when communicated to the credit card company computer file.

Calling the Dogs Off

Some clients simply cannot handle the telephone calls and pressure that the credit card companies impose on them once the payments are in arrears. When this is the case, we intervene early and notify the companies of our representation – as a means of "calling the dogs off."

We "call the dogs off" by sending a letter to each of the credit card companies and any other creditors informing them of our representation of the client. Our letter indicates that we need verification of the amount claimed by the creditor and requests that they provide to us written evidence establishing the cardmember agreement. Most of the time, the credit card company does not have a copy of the written signed card member agreement. In fact, over the last few years, many cards have been issued via online sites such that the only evidence of the agreement would be the electronic data file showing the card user's acceptance of the terms. We ask for it as a matter of course.

The cardmember agreement does pose a couple of interesting issues. Have you ever wondered how many cards have been issued improperly in the last five years when mail or email solicitations to become a card member are received by the spouse or a friend of the intended recipient? I don't know the number - but my guess is it is big. The solicitation is typically in the mail and indicates the person is "preapproved" with the only requirement to go online and insert the "approval code." When you do that, if you know the social security number of your spouse (or your friend), that is all it takes. The account application is processed online, approved (in the good old days) and the cards are mailed within a couple of days. So the legal question is what if the card is never used by the person it is issued to – instead it is used exclusively by the other spouse or friend. In this instance, I believe the credit card issuer, if challenged, cannot successfully pursue the claim. This type of suit does, however, pose some challenging issues as between the person who wrongfully obtained the account (i.e. the fraudulent perpetrator) and the actual person who the account was intended. I also see a distinction here from the situation where the card is obtained, initially without the spouse's knowledge, but subsequently the card is used by the named person to whom it is issued. In this case, the acceptance of the benefits would give rise to legal theories that would tend to favor the card issuer.

The other situation where the card member agreement comes into play is in the case where a business card is issued in the name of the business or the name of the user of the card. If, at the time of obtaining the card, the named person's social security number is provided to the issuer, the issuer typically takes the position that the individual is liable on the card as a joint user or guarantor. I always ask to see what proof the card issuer has that the individual, as opposed to the business entity, is liable on the card.

You should understand the card issuers encounter these arguments on a relatively frequent basis. They tend to simply ignore the issue and proceed forward with the normal collection process. In the current environment, where the ability to settle with the card issuers is relatively easy and inexpensive, these issues do not have great relevance. Simply put, if you're able to settle the claim in the range of 15-40%, the cost of settling is less than the cost of paying the legal expense of attempting to defend the claim on the basis that the card was never issued to you.

The letter we send to the credit card issuer or any creditor for that matter is intended to accomplish two objectives. First, to "call the dogs off," We inform them that we are attorneys acting on behalf of our client and that all further communications are to be directed through our office. We remind the creditor that they are bound by the Fair Debt Collection Practices Act[1] ("FDCPA"), as well as common law and state law governing their conduct. The second objective is to create a clear impression to the creditor that the client is suffering severe financial distress and that the likelihood of collecting on the debt is slim. We do this by indicating in the letter that our firm specializes in Financial Crisis Management, inclusive of bankruptcy and emphasize that the client is undergoing severe economic distress. We indicate that we have been engaged for the purpose of assisting the client through the best and most effective method of relieving the financial hardship they face and that we are evaluating the file in this context. We use the "bankruptcy" word because credit card companies are large institutions. As soon as that word is used, most credit card companies assume this means we will be filing a bankruptcy for the client on a short term basis, and, as such,

---

[1] Technically, the FDCPA only applies to third party collectors, but I make the same claim and warning to the credit card issuers.

the file is then categorized as highly unlikely to make a recovery. This is precisely what we want them to think – but at the same time – we have not represented to them that we will be filing bankruptcy or that we have been retained to specifically file a bankruptcy. To me this is significant, because while I indorse aggressive and relentless representation of a client's interests, I also believe that, as an attorney, you have an obligation not to misstate the facts and to be accurate in the statements and commitments you make. The distinction lies in the words selected. While the creditor will in most instances misunderstand the point and assume we're going to file bankruptcy – that is the creditor's problem and we are not their mother's keeper! If playing specificity seems a bit Clintonish to some of you, I can only say that our job, as attorneys representing the person who faces financial crisis, is to vigorously represent them within the confines of the law. When you compare the credit card industry's history of notifying you of a change in the card agreement terms by sending you a 3,000 word revised version of the card member agreement in 8 point font and not even identifying the specific changes, I submit to you that we are being more than fair! (Too bad for the credit card company!)

The Negotiations

After the letter is received by the credit card company and the phone calls start coming to my office, the first two questions often asked are, "What is the case number for the bankruptcy?" and, "What Chapter are they filing?" When I hear these questions, I'm always amused. I could reply by saying, "Didn't you read my letter? We haven't made any of those determinations or a determination as to what type of case it is." Of course I could say that – but I don't! I know if they hear Chapter 7 that fact will incentivize them to settle for less money than in a Chapter 13. So the key for us is, how do we respond so that they hear what we want them to hear (given their stupidity) but we do not misstate what is happening? Typically, this is what I say: "Mr. Jones has not filed bankruptcy yet. We are waiting on paperwork and he has not yet paid us for a bankruptcy filing. As to the Chapter – all I can tell you at this stage is that unless you have steady income sufficient to pay your bills, you're not eligible to file a Chapter 13. I can tell you, Mr. Jones does not have the income needed to support his obligations." If they ask more, we tell them, "Once we get the paperwork and money from the client, then we will be in a position to answer your questions."

The entire strategy here is to create the clear impression to the credit card company that they are not going to get paid no matter what they do.

The calling and settlement process that we employ is constantly updated and revised based upon changes in the credit card landscape and the position we find each of the specific card companies are taking. The process typically works like this. After the client has either taken the calls for 30 to 45 days following the first missed payments, we send each of the credit card companies the letter advising them of our representation. At that stage, we wait for the calls to start coming in. The calls are directed to one of the attorneys who takes the calls and makes it clear to the creditor that there is little likelihood they are going to collect the debt.

Normally, we make each creditor call back at least three to five times before we begin speaking with them. We inform the creditor that our firm represents many people, all who are in serious financial crisis, and the plain fact of the matter is that we don't have the time to talk to them except in the rare circumstance that there is something that can be accomplished. On the first couple of calls, we indicate that we are waiting on paperwork, that the client is in terrible financial distress and there is nothing to discuss in terms of settlement. We are always nice, though sometimes firm, because the creditors are often unhappy that we will not discuss settlement with them - (too bad for them!). We tell them that we would prefer that they do not call back for at least 30 days, but that if they must call back sooner, we will update them on the status. This same process is repeated for three to five calls. At the point where the creditor is getting antsy and, or annoyed, is when we begin the first phase to settle the account. My rule of thumb is that I try to avoid talking to the creditor until they have come down to 40% - 50% of the amount claimed. We get there using the creditor's frustration at not being able to speak with us. The positioning here is to psychologically get them to think they must reach deep in making an offer once they are able to speak about settlement with us. From my perspective, this is "fun" because I enjoy creating a process that they fall into. To me, it's like taking a shot back at them for all the sneaky, underhanded garbage they have put on all of us all of these years. Keep in mind, this strategy does not always work. When it doesn't, we employ alternative approaches.

Once the credit card representative makes an offer, we indicate to them that we will look at the offer and get back to them in the next couple of days. The credit card representative always wants to conclude matters right away and, in many cases, they only have a limited number of days to resolve the account, otherwise it passes to another collection group, which can be an internal or external third party collector. Here is when it gets interesting. In most cases, the person who is speaking for the credit card company is paid a commission on the settlement and has a fixed deadline as to the amount of time he or she has to "work the file." The cycle in which they must settle the account typically ends during the last week of the calendar month. It is in this window that the best deals can be cut. If possible, we try to set the stage in the third week so that there is room to negotiate and have the credit card representative come down to give us the best deal. The first call with the representative is not the time to settle. We tell them that we have several deals with other card issuers in the works and that we will not settle any of them unless everyone comes down to 10% - 15%. We then tell the representative that their number is way too high and to call us back if they really want to make a deal. We're cordial on the phone, but we give the clear impression that we are pessimistic as to making a deal and that we do not want to stay on the phone. The representative wants to earn a commission and tries hard to keep us on the phone and point out the benefits of the transaction. I often hear, "Mr. Gross, a 40% discount is very generous and far better than we give to our other clients. You should accept this while you have the opportunity." My reply is typically, "Listen, do you think I'm a Debt Settlement company that takes the first offer and sells his client down the river. I'm an attorney trying to help these people through extreme financial problems. Please, with all respect, let's not waste each other's time." I then typically say, "I've told the client it is in their best interest to file bankruptcy and discharge the debt and that I don't want to waste your time (the representative's) or mine, so if you can't come down we don't have anything to talk about." This little chit chat back and forth usually results in the representative lowering his offer down to the 20% - 45% range. Depending on the creditor, we meet this offer with little enthusiasm and tell the representative that he can call us back in the next couple of days if they want to lower their offer. We end the call at this stage. The call normally ends politely, if the representative knows when to stop talking, and other times, with a curt, "Listen, I have told you where we're at on this file and I have no reason to stay on the line; feel free to call if you want to settle the account." The tenor of the calls is not static. If we've spoken with the same representative on other files or if we know the offer is in the expected range for this creditor, then the discussions are more cordial because we are on track to successfully conclude the settlement.

Usually the card collector calls back the next day. We continue to try and work them down and do not give an inclination to conclude the process. The process can go on a couple of more calls, but once we get to the 23rd to 25th day of the month, the effort to settle gets more intense and that is when we try to cut the deal. Keep in mind, the best way to negotiate any matter, is to be willing to walk away and say, "No." Nothing in negotiation is more powerful than the willingness and ability to say no. When we take on these engagements, we review the process with the client. Typically, they look to us to decide if the offer should be accepted but the ultimate decision rests with the client. Another great negotiation point is that in negotiations you can always say, "No" and then call back the next day and rekindle the negotiation process. This is different than poker, where you have to call the hand in order to maintain your bluff. In negotiations, you can say "no" and then turn around the next day and start anew.

Keep in mind, the best way to negotiate any matter, is to be willing to walk away and say, "No." Nothing in negotiation is more powerful than the willingness and ability to say no.

Once we have an acceptable number – which is a percentage of the total debt, we then typically tell the representative that we don't have the cash and must have at least six months to make the payments. We tell them six, knowing that the most they will probably allow is four months and many times they want the payment in three monthly payments. Sometimes they respond by saying that if we wanted payments, we should have told them upfront because then the best they can do is only reduce the amount by 50%. Well – when I hear this, I want to say, "Listen Nimrod, if I told you that then I wouldn't have you at 25% now would I?" Of course, I don't say that. Instead I say, "Listen; there's nothing I can do. They don't have the money, but I've gone through their budget and they can make the payments. Unless you can tell me where to print money, there's nothing I can do." This dialogue usually results in a payment agreement calling for four payments over three months.

The last step in gaining a settlement with the credit card companies almost always involves the supervisor. Remember what I said, it's the supervisor who approves the deal. We often end up speaking to the supervisor, because we hold tight at 15-20% on the settlement and at the end, the representative, who wants to make the commission, submits the offer to his supervisor and attempts to get it approved. Here is where reading the file comes in. The supervisor reviews the file. If it's approved, we don't hear from him (or her) and the representative comes back on the line or calls us back and we have a deal. If the supervisor will not approve the deal, our next conversation is usually with him and they are explaining to us why they cannot go as low as we want. This is an important conversation. We need to know if there is anything in the "file" that is causing a problem and we need to determine what is going to happen to the file in the short term if no settlement is obtained. Sometimes, the supervisor will tell us that there were several "cash advances" on the card shortly before the default and that the company looks at these in a harsher tone and therefore they can't go down to 15% or 20%. More often, however, my experience is that the supervisor is just being a hard ass and wants more money. We then try to find out what will happen during the next month with the file. We say to him, "Well they simply don't have the money now to make that deal; there's nothing we can do. Will this file stay with you next month or go to another group?" Typically, if the file is still with the issuer, they might say, "the file will be charged off at the end of the month." If the account is more than 4-5 months behind, a big question is whether it's going to a third party collector, a local attorney to file suit or whether it will head to limbo land for a while. We always try hard to establish a solid rapport with the supervisor and find out as much information about the internal process of the particular credit card company or the third party collection firm.

Should We Take the Deal?

The decision as to whether to accept or decline, in my view comes down to two issues. First, if we are doing Debt Resolution we have already decided that the game plan for the client is not to file bankruptcy. We therefore need to settle the case at what we believe is the most optimal point. As long as the account remains in the hands of the credit card issuer or a third party collector, we know there is more time available and the offers will at least stay the same and sometimes get better. The cutoff point for us is to reach a settlement before the account is sent to a local attorney to file suit. My experience in the last two to three years indicates that the settlements obtained through the attorneys are not as good. If the file ends up with an attorney then there is pressure to settle in order to avoid having to defend the lawsuit.

This is an issue people often do not understand. What happens if the credit card company or any creditor sues you? Do you need to do something? What can happen? Too often people do get sued and ignore the papers. When you are sued, you must be served with a Summons and a Complaint. In most jurisdictions, this requires that you either accept a certified mailing of the documents or that you are served personally with the papers by a process server. Once "service" has occurred, you have anywhere between 20 and 30 days in most states to file an "Answer" to the Complaint. If you do that, the court process continues for a time until there is either a trial or the matter is concluded as a result of the creditor filing a motion for summary judgment or summary disposition prior to the trial date.

If you ignore the papers and do not file an Answer, either on your own or with the assistance of an attorney, the creditor, who is the "Plaintiff" in the lawsuit will obtain a default judgment against you. Shortly thereafter (after the time period to file and appeal lapses, typically 21 days) the creditor can then seek to garnish wages or attach your property in an effort to collect the judgment. This is not a good thing and this is a situation that you want to avoid. First and foremost, if the lawsuit stage comes and you do nothing, you lose your bargaining position if the creditor gets the judgment against you. By answering the lawsuit, you buy more time to negotiate and you cause the creditor (or the creditor's attorney) more costs and time in ultimately trying to collect from you. *For this reason, we never let clients ignore lawsuits and have default judgments taken against them.* The only exception to this rule is where we have already decided to file bankruptcy and the case will be filed before the creditor can cause any problems.

So in the Debt Resolution arena, if we don't settle the case before it ends up in the hands of an attorney, the next part of the plan will require us to either settle with the attorney or defend the lawsuit. You might ask, "Can't I defend myself?" The answer is yes – but I don't advise it. The process is too complicated and taking on that process puts you at a disadvantage from the standpoint of settlement. Attorneys work with attorneys. For instance, in Metro Detroit, we know practically every collection attorney because we deal with them on a regular basis. They are not the enemy – it is their clients that are. When I have a lawsuit come in, I will call the attorney, shoot the breeze with him or her for a bit and find out what is the "best possible" deal they can get this particular creditor to go along with. The collection attorney's motivation is to close cases quickly and that trumps the goal of maximizing the amount collected on any one file. Thus, the strategy at this stage is to find out what the best deal is and then make it. Keep in mind, Debt Resolution is a strategy for someone that has cash flow and too much credit card debt. We are freeing up the money that was being used to pay the credit cards and using it to fund the settlements and any necessary legal costs incurred. If you have no money and no income, Debt Resolution is not the strategy to use in the first instance. Additionally, if we are in the mode where we need to actually defend the case, we can then assert claims, which challenge the creditor's ability to actually produce the card member agreement and the validity of the debt charged.

So, if a creditor ends up suing you, the plan is to defend the suit, buying time to reach the best settlement with the plaintiff's attorney. The trick, which requires finesse and experience, is figuring out when to settle the accounts before they land in the lawsuit stage. If, however, the lawsuit ensues, the strategy is to buy time and then use that leverage to settle. I know, you may be saying to yourself, "Geez, this is complicated, I don't want to be sued." I understand this thought but want you to resist it. The goal of preserving your future income for your family and your retirement and not paying the debts of the past (since no one is returning the assets you've lost) is a solid, smart goal. Just because the process is not as simple as pie - you should not, I repeat, you should not - allow them to deter you from pursuing what could well be the most important decision of your future.

Debt Settlement Companies

Debt Settlement and the services offered by the so-called "Debt Settlement Companies" is similar to Debt Resolution but there are major differences. First and foremost, Debt Settlement Companies are one of those "new businesses" that have emerged during the Financial Crisis along with the proliferation of "loan modification" and "short sale experts." I'm not a fan of these companies for a couple of reasons. First of all, the only service they offer is Debt Settlement, which means they are going to attempt to sell you on their service as the cure all, fix all, save all solution for your life. If they don't sell you, they don't do any business. They are biased from the beginning because other solutions, which may be in your best interest, are not in their interest. To me, this is a big problem. Another major issue to me is that you are engaging them to settle your debts with the credit card companies but you have no idea what skills they bring to the table. You can be sure they are not attorneys. What do they know about negotiation? Can they effectively threaten bankruptcy when they are not capable of representing the client in a bankruptcy? Can they challenge the credit card issuer's right to enforce the cardmember agreement? Have they analyzed the tax consequences of the plan and made an informed decision for you as to the total cost, inclusive of taxes, of settling the debt?

First of all, the only service they offer is Debt Settlement, which means they are going to attempt to sell you on their service as the cure all, fix all, save all solution for your life. If they don't sell you, they don't do any business. They are biased from the beginning because other solutions, which may be in your best interest, are not in their interest.

My point is that right off the bat – these companies lack the leverage that is critical in gaining the best settlement. There is a big difference between settling a $20,000 credit card debt for 50% compared to 15%. In the macro view, this is the difference between ultimate success and failure of the program. Keep in mind, my goal in Debt Resolution is to use the money that was being paid monthly on the cards to settle the debt over time. If the settlements are not as low as possible, there simply will not be sufficient funds to take advantage of the settlements.

One of the absolute biggest problems I have with the Debt Settlement companies are that if you are sued – they are not attorneys and they cannot defend you in the lawsuit. You cannot simply allow a judgment to be taken against you. This is a mistake that should never occur.

Pricing is also an issue. This issue depends on the fees being charged by both the Debt Settlement Company and by the attorney who is providing you Debt Resolution services. In our practice, we have priced Debt Resolution on a fixed fee basis tied to the amount of the debt and in our experience the total fees paid by the client are far less than to the Debt Settlement companies. Most Debt Settlement companies charge a fee equal to 15% - 18% of the total debt, plus monthly service fees of $85 - $95 per month. Most settlements by Debt Settlement companies are in the 50% range (i.e. if the credit card balance is $8,000, the settlement is $4,000). For a client with $100,000 of debt, if the debt is ultimately settled at 50%, the fee in this instance is $15,000, plus monthly fees of $1,800, for a total cost, inclusive of the settlement of $66,800 – which is 66.8% of the original debt. On top of that, without proper planning, you could be faced with tax consequences on $50,000, representing the amount of debt canceled on the settlements.

Debt Settlement companies often require you to pay the amount you would pay on the cards to the company monthly which is held in a segregated account for settlement and you authorize the company to settle in their discretion from the fund, with the understanding they can take their fee from the fund as well. I do not like this arrangement. First of all, the Debt Settlement Company does not have sufficient incentive to fight for the best deals. When an offer to settle at 50% comes, they can simply accept the offer. In the end, it's costing you 66%, which is not an acceptable settlement in virtually all circumstances. This situation happens with far too great frequency with the result that the client's funds are usurped too quickly on the first couple of settlements. In this situation, the Debt Settlement company stops working on the client's behalf and the unsettled debt remains. Too often, the next phase is the client is being served papers for lawsuits from the credit card companies and then must seek help from others to solve their problems.

There have been numerous complaints filed with the Federal Trade Commission as to the abuses and practices of the Debt Settlement Industry. It is not my intention to trash the entire industry. I'm sure there are some responsible and established providers of this service out there. My advice is that before you even pursue Debt Settlement, you need to determine if this is one of the correct components in the overall goal of shedding debt. You will not be able to determine this by talking to the Debt Settlement Company. Hopefully, this book will help give you that guidance, as well as finding someone to review the matter that is versed in Financial Crisis Management and all of its tools.

Of significance, as well, is the distinction and protections you receive when you use the services of licensed professionals compared to the lack of protections when you don't. Attorneys and certified public accountants are licensed by the state they practice in. If they fail to abide by the rules of professional conduct dictated by their profession, there are strict consequences that attach to disciplinary actions that can be initiated by the state acting on the complaint of an aggrieved party. In the unlicensed arena, where debt settlement providers and loan modifiers reside, there is no such protection.

Remember the "Wild, Wild West?" Well - I do from television and the movies and my advice to you is not to vest your future strategy with people who can come and go with the wind.

By contrast, my concept of Debt Resolution is that the service should be provided by an attorney. When I say this, I don't mean by a Debt Settlement company that pretends to be a law firm but is really only providing debt settlement services and engages low paid clerks and assistants to handle the files. When I say attorneys, I mean you should be dealing with a licensed attorney in all material aspects of the engagement.

Additionally, the right attorney is well versed in negotiation. The difference between settling these accounts at 40% to 60% compared to 15% to 40% lies in the talent and strategy employed in the negotiation process. As far as cost goes, I can't speak for all attorneys. We charge a flat 7.5% of the debt existing at the time of the engagement. There are no monthly fees or additional costs. Typically, we also provide the defense of lawsuits, if they arise, at no additional cost. You may find the fee structure to be higher in your area. Our experience and passion in this arena makes it feasible for us to provide the high level of service at these rates. Those attorneys with less experience in this arena, may be reluctant to provide flat fee engagements of this nature. My advice is that you look carefully at the experience of the attorney you engage as well as the fee structure they are proposing. Keep in mind; this is not an "Official Guide." I'm providing it to you so that you have a basis to review proposals you may receive from persons contacted to provide this assistance.

9

Tax Relief and Tax Issues

Okay – let's talk about everyone's least favorite subject and most hated agency. Take a wild stab. The subject – taxes. The agency – the Internal Revenue Service – IRS. For some, anxiety ensues by the mere mention of the words. For others - anger or passive indifference is the reaction. Regardless of the emotions, we all know the old adage that there is no escaping death and taxes. Death is an absolute truth and I can tell you that *Dump Your Debt* does not have a chapter or theory on how to avoid that eventuality (though I do have some ideas on how to prolong the inevitable). When it comes to taxes, it is true that you cannot avoid the existence of taxes and your obligations to pay, but there are circumstances where you can sometimes successfully discharge or reduce your existing tax liability.

Additionally, there are steps and procedures that you can follow in order to obtain time to pay past due tax bills so that you do not have to live in fear of having your bank account or wages levied without notice.

One of the most troubling tax issues that people in financial crisis face is the circumstance where the government taxes you on "forgiveness of debt." This situation arises with short sales, deeds in lieu of foreclosure, foreclosure and Debt Resolution. The problem is that under several situations, where the creditor receives less than was originally loaned, the difference can give rise to income tax consequences to the individual – and this occurs at a time where the money does not exist to pay the tax. The good news is that there are exceptions to this rule, but some of them take some planning - so you need to pay attention. This is an area that I find the media and commentators do not give enough attention – so this is my attempt to provide you the information that is needed to make the proper decisions. After all, how much good does it do you if we are successful at eliminating $75,000 of debt through Debt Resolution, but at the year-end you receive 1099s from the creditors and your accountant tells you that you must pay tax on the $75,000? The answer – well it's still good, but not that good and now you have a new problem. Taxes due and no money! Worse yet, if you have an IRA or 401(k), those assets are not reachable by any creditor except one – Uncle Sam – when it comes to collection of taxes.

In this chapter, we're going to address the key tax issues when it comes to Financial Crisis Management. Those issues are:

- If the creditor receives less that it is owed, is the difference taxable to me?

- How to address unfiled tax returns and unpaid taxes

- What is an Offer in Compromise?

- What is the process to defer IRS from collecting taxes owed?

When is Forgiveness of Debt Income?

The best way to begin this rather annoying section is to set out the general rule as stated by the IRS in its *Publication 4681, Canceled Debts, Foreclosures, Repossessions and Abandonments* (you can find this at www.irs.gov/pub/irs-pdf/p4681.pdf). Here it is:

"Generally, if you owe a debt to someone else and they cancel or forgive that debt, you are treated for income taxes as having income and may have to pay tax on this income."

You are probably thinking this is ridiculous. How can I pay tax when I'm not getting any money to pay the taxes? I share this sentiment and to some extent our friends and foes in the IRS and Congress recognize that this can be a significant problem. Let's examine briefly why it is considered income. The rationale goes like this. When you receive the credit – either through the use of credit cards or borrowing from the bank for a mortgage loan – the money received is not income because it is a loan. Your obligation is to repay the loan so it is not income. On the other hand, if the money you just received did not come from a loan but instead you won it at the racetrack or in a lottery, in that case it is not a surprise that it is treated as income. This is where the tax aspect comes into play. When the debt is canceled, it is the same as if you won the money at the racetrack or lottery, except, in the cancelation situation, the victory comes later when the money is not there. The notion that money you receive is taxable when you receive it with no obligation to repay (other than a gift) is not difficult to comprehend. We understand that winnings at the track or from a slot machine give rise to income. Cancelation of a debt yields the same result. The difference is in the timing because the cancelation of the debt is the taxable event but you don't have the money that you received. Gifts, on the other hand, in contrast to gambling winnings or a lottery are not considered income. The distinction rests with the person making the gift – if that person is detached and disinterested and makes the gift with no expectation in return then it is not income. The same would be true if that same person made a loan and then elected to forgive it to you. For example, if your parents loaned you money to buy a home and then, from the kindness of their heart elected to cancel the debt, that event could qualify as a gift and there would be no income tax consequence. When a bank, however, cancels the remaining credit card balance on a settlement or forgives the balance of debt owed on a mortgage, that transaction is not related to the kindness of the bank's heart and it therefore does not meet the standards needed to be considered a gift.

In the housing sector with foreclosures, as well as repossessions for property such as vehicles, there are two events that actually occur from a tax standpoint. The foreclosure or repossession is treated as a sale which can require you to realize gain or loss on the transaction. Typically, there is little in the way of gain realized in a foreclosure or repossession, so we will not dwell on this point. The second event, however, is significant. According to the IRS, if the outstanding loan balance was more than the FMV of the property and the lender cancels all or part of the remaining loan balance, you realize ordinary income from this cancelation of debt. You must report this income on your return unless certain exceptions or exclusions apply.

The dreaded IRS Form that reports these events is the 1099-C. A lender is required to file Form 1099-C and send you a copy if the canceled debt is $600 or more and the lender is a financial institution, credit union, federal government agency or any organization that has a significant trade or business of lending money. Looking at the bright side, if you've defaulted on your second mortgage to Uncle Leo, at least he is not required to file the 1099-C. (Of course, this does not mean that you can ignore the income tax consequences, if they exist; only that the IRS will not learn of the event from Uncle Leo).

So now the stage is set. The bad news is that the canceled debt, whether it is from a credit card, short sale or foreclosure, will generate a 1099-C and you will have to report the income on your taxes unless there is an exception. The good news is that there are three major exceptions that help to eliminate the requirement that you report the canceled debt as income. The exceptions do not work in every situation so you need to be sure to analyze this issue in the planning and operational plan of your Financial Crisis Management strategy.

Exception #1 – Bankruptcy Filing

The first exception is the biggest, broadest and easiest. If you file for bankruptcy protection canceled debt is not included in income. The only conditions are that if you file a Chapter 7, the case must be completed to discharge (the normal course) or if a Chapter 13 or Chapter 11, the plan must be approved. The existence of this exception emphasizes the benefits of the bankruptcy laws. To me, it serves as a reminder, that when it comes to achieving the goal of preserving future income and avoiding payment of debts of the past that the bankruptcy laws are an excellent and inexpensive tool. People are well served to overcome the anxiety and notion that bankruptcy must be avoided at all costs. The point here is that if the consequences of Cancelation of Debt give rise to tax obligations that could otherwise be avoided by a bankruptcy filing, then that alternative must be looked at. The situation will depend on the circumstances but it is safe to say, that if our goal is to shed debt and preserve future income, we certainly do not want any unneeded tax obligations incurred for the benefit of good old Uncle Sam!

Exception #2 – Qualified Principal Residence Indebtedness

The Emergency Economic Stabilization Act of 2008 extended the Mortgage Debt Relief Act of 2007 and provides for an exclusion of income from the discharge of debt on your principal residence if the debt is forgiven after 2006 and before the end of 2012.

The debt that can be excluded is called "Qualified Principal Residence Indebtedness." It includes "any debt incurred in acquiring, constructing, or substantially improving your principal residence and which is secured by your principal residence." (Page 7, IRS Publication 4681). Refinanced debt is also included up to the amount of the debt refinanced or to the extent that additional money is obtained from a refinance for improvements to the residence. If, however, you refinanced to pull money out to pay off credit cards and other non-housing items then that money is not excluded under this exception. This is an important exception – if you refinanced the home and pulled money out to pay off credit card bills – that portion of the debt does not meet the Qualified Principal Residence Exclusion and the exclusion on Canceled Debt does not apply to the extent of that debt. The IRS calls this the "Ordering Rule." This rule provides that when there is a refinance and some of the money was used to pay down other debt, that amount is not eligible for the exclusion under this exception.

There are two other limitations that come into play with this exception. The maximum exclusion is $1 million per individual and $2 million if married filing a joint return. Also, this exclusion only applies to your principal residence, which is defined as "the home where you ordinarily live most of the time" (IRS Publication 4681, Page 7-8). You are also only permitted to have one principal residence at any one time. So to recap – the Qualified Principal Residence exclusion covers:

QUALIFIED PRINCIPAL RESIDENCE EXCLUSION FROM CANCELED DEBT INCOME	
Eligible Years	Debt Discharged After 2006 and before 2013
Maximum Exclusion	$1 Million Per Individual $2 Million for Married filing joint
Excluded Debt	Debts that are incurred in acquiring, constructing, or substantially improving your principal residence that are secured by your principal residence
Not Excluded	Amounts refinanced to pay down credit cards and other bills

So what if you are not filing bankruptcy and you are going to be receiving a 1099-C from a lender arising from canceled debt on a short sale where all or a portion of the debt was not eligible for this exclusion or from a credit card settlement? Must you pay income taxes on this so-called income even though you have no money? Well, all is not yet lost. There is another exception and it is called the Insolvency Exclusion.

Exception #3 – Insolvency Exclusion

This is a big exclusion and often, but not always, covers the problem. You do not include a canceled debt as income *to the extent you were insolvent immediately before the cancelation.* The calculation is easy. You add all the fair market value of all of your assets – *including retirement accounts (IRAs and 401(k) accounts, etc.)* and all property you own. Now add all liabilities (debts), including credit cards, mortgages, medical bills, student loans, past due interest on loans, judgments, loans on insurance policies, margin debt, etc. To the extent your liabilities exceed your assets; you are "Insolvent." If the total amount you are insolvent is $100,000 and the credit card companies cancel $60,000 of your credit card debts, you will not have to report the $60,000 as income because you are permitted to exclude up to $100,000. If however, the total amount the banks and credit card companies canceled was $110,000, then you are maxed out at $100,000 and the additional $10,000 must be reported as income.

The end result of this rule is that to the extent that after the cancelation of the debt your assets exceed your liabilities, you will have income to the extent of the excess subject to a maximum equal to the amount of canceled debt. Take the above example, before the debt is canceled, you were insolvent by $100,000. Because the debt that was canceled is $110,000, you are now positive, or solvent, by $10,000. You must therefore pick up $10,000 of income and can only exclude $100,000.

An interesting issue that arises in the Insolvency Exclusion analysis and in the Bankruptcy Exclusion analysis is whether the taxpayer can include in the liabilities the amount of a debt that the taxpayer has guaranteed. Typically, this situation arises when the taxpayer's business has loans outstanding which he has given his personal guaranty to the bank. Another scenario is where a person guarantees an auto or other loan on behalf of a family member or a friend (this by the way, is *never* a good idea!). The law considers a guaranteed debt as a contingent liability. The critical factor here, from the standpoint of the tax consequences on the exclusion, is whether it was more likely than not that they would be required to pay the liability when dealing with a contingent liability. In Tax Court cases addressing this rule, the Court has ruled against the taxpayer in circumstances where the taxpayer failed to prove it was more likely they would have been required to pay the liability. This is another important planning point that is often ignored.

You Can Use More than One Exclusion

Suppose you did refinance your home and pull money out to pay off credit card debt? In this case, you can still use the Qualified Principal Residence Exclusion on the non-refinanced portion of canceled debt and then apply the remaining portion against the Insolvency Exclusion to see if you can exclude all or a portion of the remainder.

To claim the exclusion from income, you must report the exclusion on IRS Form 982 and attach it to your return. Part 1 of the form is required to be completed and it is a simple form.

The bottom line is simply that the tax issue is a material issue that must be evaluated and planned for in the context of eliminating debt and preserving future income. In many situations, the recognition of canceled debt as income is a non-issue. In situations where you're not filing bankruptcy, the issue requires you to run through a few critical questions to evaluate the issue:

SCOPING OUT THE ISSUE – CANCELATION OF DEBT AS INCOME ANALYSIS		
1	Is a Short Sale or Deed in Lieu of Foreclosure at Issue?	Need to watch for Cancelation of Debt Income if you refinanced the home and pulled money out to pay credit card bills, etc.
2	Has the Mortgage Lender Reduced the Principal or Canceled the Remaining Debt?	(Same as Above)

3	If Question 1 or 2, above apply, and you did not refinance -	Then if this is your Primary Residence and the cancelation occurs after 2006 and before 2013 you're protected under the Qualified Principal Residence Exclusion up to $2 Million for Married Filing Joint and $1 Million for an Individual
4	Have you received Canceled Debt from a Credit Card lender or a lender other than your Mortgage Lender on Your Primary Residence?	Then you will be protected if you file for Bankruptcy Protection;[2] otherwise, you need to analyze the Insolvency Exclusion
5	You Have Received Canceled Debt and you're not filing Bankruptcy and it does not qualify for the Qualified Principal Residence Exclusion – so you need to analyze the Insolvency Exclusion	Calculate your Total Assets and subtract your Total Liabilities immediately prior to the cancelation - if negative, you are Insolvent. Income is Excluded Up to the Amount You are Insolvent

Cancelation of Debt as income is not the only arena in which the IRS rears its head in the arena of Financial Crisis Management. Let's next focus on addressing the issue of what do you need to do and what can you do when you have tax debt and you are facing the collection branch of the IRS.

---

[2] You still must be careful of Contingent Liability issues as to Exclusion from Income Tax

Facing the IRS – Such Fun!

So you owe taxes – or perhaps you owe taxes and have not filed tax returns. It is not the end of the world. At the same time, it can be a cause of enormous stress and anxiety particularly when the situation is not in a controlled context. Believe it or not, it does not have to be this way. There are many steps that can be taken to gain control of the situation. The situations we see are typically one of three. For one of many reasons, a person has failed to file his or her tax return for one or for several years. Also common is the problem where the tax returns have been filed, but there is an outstanding balance due the taxing authority and the taxpayer needs assistance in addressing this issue. The third most common tax related problem we encounter is the situation where a business owner has failed to make sure that the company they own has paid its employment taxes on its employees.

Problems such as these have solutions. The first key is addressing the issues and gaining control of the situation so that you know where you are going and how you are going to get there. I have a golden rule on matters such as these – it applies in all three of these situations and any other situation where you alone are facing the power and size of government:

GOLDEN RULE – NEVER, NEVER, NEVER REPRESENT YOURSELF BEFORE THE IRS OR ANY GOVERNMENT AGENCY THAT IS SEEKING TO COLLECT MONEY FROM YOU.

This rule is critical and I don't care who you are. Whether you're a lawyer, an accountant, a certified public accountant or the person who wrote the tax code - you should never represent yourself in this situation. There are several reasons – but the most critical one is deniability. An example illustrates the issue best. Suppose you owe the IRS $30,000 in back taxes and you've received a Final Notice of Intent to Levy. You decide to take action and call the 800 number on the notice. You are now speaking to a person in the IRS Automated Collection System. You don't know what they are authorized to do or what terms they can offer you to pay the tax over time. More importantly, if you're speaking to them and trying to work out a payment arrangement, it shouldn't come as a surprise to you if they want to ask you information. For example, suppose Mr. IRS asks you, "Where do you bank? What are the account numbers on your checking and savings account? Are there any customers who owe you money? If so, what are the names and address of these customers?" All of these questions are questions that unless you are suffering from a severe memory deficit disorder, you would know the answer and you would feel incredibly uncomfortable on the phone or at a meeting with an IRS Collection Officer telling him, "I'm sorry, I can't remember where I bank, the account numbers or whether I have any customers who owe me money." At the same time, however, this is the *last* information you want them to have, particularly when you don't even know if they will allow you payment terms that you can afford. Once you give out this information, it is logged into the IRS system and they can immediately send out levies on your bank accounts and to your customers directing them to pay the money to the IRS! This is precisely why you always need a representative – even if you're a lawyer or an accountant!

Take this situation. If I'm representing Mr. Smith, the taxpayer, and I call IRS Automated Collections or meet with a collection officer the situation is totally different. Not because I'm a magician, but because I have the ability to not know information that the client cannot reasonably claim to not know. When the IRS representative asks me about Mr. Smith's bank accounts and customers, I can simply say, "I don't know that information. If you need it, I'll have to get with the client and get back to you. In the meantime, can we review the file and see what we can work out here?" Do you see the distinction? It is a critical point.

Of course, there are dozens of other reasons why you should have a professional representing you in this situation – we know what can and cannot be accomplished, we are not intimidated by the government and we know when to push for a better deal. The Golden Rule is that no one should ever put themselves in the position of representing themselves in this situation because you lose the buffer zone a professional creates to allow room for deniability or delay.

Now let's explore a couple of the most common problem areas and see what can be accomplished.

I have not filed my tax returns!

This can be a big problem – but it is the easiest to solve. It's a big problem because the failure to file a federal income tax return is a crime. Prosecutions are rare – but on occasion they do occur and they arise when it is the IRS who comes looking for you. Where a taxpayer who has not filed, "voluntarily" brings him or herself into compliance by filing the past due returns, I have never heard of a prosecution. What does this mean? I find that it is important to *spell it out for the client – particularly in situations where they are embarrassed for having gotten themselves into the situation and their brains then tend to misfire as to the necessary steps to take.* So I will spell it out for you – if you have not filed your returns –

ALL YOU NEED TO DO IS FILE THE RETURNS!

It is that simple! Once the returns are filed (before any form of criminal investigation is commenced against you) there is no longer anything to worry about from a prosecution standpoint.

The Feds do not come to the door to arrest you for filing the return late! The IRS is bad at times - but they are not that bad!

I know – you have questions. The first one is usually- How can I file the return, I don't know where the records are or they are such a mess I can't get it done? The Answer – if necessary, estimate the information. The key is to file the return. If the IRS audits it, then you will deal with record issues, etc. – but the criminal aspect is eliminated. Next question – "I don't have the money to pay, so shouldn't I hold off on filing the return until I have the money? Answer – **NO! NO! NO!** Payment of the tax is a separate issue. We do not have "debtor's prison" in the United States. It is not criminal if you do not pay –it is criminal if you do not file. So let's get the returns filed and then we can explore your options in paying or resolving the tax debt.

Can I Compromise the Tax Debt?

For many years, the air waves have been bombarded by television and radio commercials from nationally advertised and so-called "tax experts" that have professed to be able to settle your IRS tax debt for pennies on the dollar. Ronnie Deutch, Tax Masters and JK Harris were among the biggest advertisers of such claims. If you haven't noticed, all three of them are no longer in business. All three were either forced out of business or closed down as part of the bankruptcy process amidst enforcement actions against them for fraudulent marketing practices.

Companies of this nature work like this. They have large marketing budgets to generate calls into their call center. They play fast and loose with the truth in their advertising in order to get you to call. When you do call, the phone is not answered by a lawyer or certified public accountant that *listens to your problem and then makes a professional assessment as to whether they can help you.* Instead, the call is taken by a "representative" or "account representative" who is really nothing more than a commissioned sales representative whose only goal is to get you to hire the firm by telling you virtually anything that will make you feel good enough to part with your credit card number. The end result is unfortunate. Thousands of people in need of assistance have been fleeced out of their money. After paying substantial fees, they learn six months to a year later that these companies did absolutely nothing to resolve the problem. Unfortunately, these companies typically file what are known as Offers in Compromise in circumstances that the taxpayer does not meet the criteria. They also request Collection Due Process hearings or short term holds on collection, which only delay the process but do not resolve the tax liability. When these processes complete, the pressure to collect the tax continues, but these tax relief companies claim their role is complete based upon the terms of their retention agreement.

The problem lies in the nature of the business model. The marketing costs of these companies are substantial. To compensate, they charge fees that are higher than necessary and in excess of what a qualified professional would actually charge. Worse yet, they skimp on labor costs by engaging "Enrolled Agents" as the person who is assigned to handle your case rather than a bonafide attorney or certified public accountant. You can become an Enrolled Agent if you properly complete a form, have no outstanding tax forms or liabilities and pass a three part Special Enrollment Examination. It is not a heavy burden and the marketing practices of these companies lead people to conclude that the "Enrolled Agent" has a level of sophistication and professionalism on par with licensed attorneys and CPAs. Understand, I'm not saying that every "Enrolled Agent" is unqualified or engages in improper conduct – but I am pointing out that these companies have been taken to task by proper authorities with the result that they are no longer around. In my view, it was the business model that was doomed from the inception because its emphasis is on "sales" and not on providing qualified professional service. It wouldn't matter if every representative was an attorney or CPA – if they operated under such a model, your interests would not be paramount.

No doubt, there will be newcomers to this industry that continue these type of practices and you should keep your guard up and avoid the temptation to be "sucked" in by their slick marketing promises. If the promise is "too good to be true" – then it probably is not true!

I do have some good news to share. On May 21, 2012, the IRS announced major changes to the Offer in Compromise Rules. At long last, these changes make it far more possible to compromise tax than under the old law. Before going into the changes, you need to understand what an Offer in Compromise ("OIC") is. For starters, it's not a "give and take" type of negotiation where we call the IRS and say, "Hey, this taxpayer is a really good person but doesn't have any money, has a hardship and is facing bankruptcy, please take a $1,000 and call it a day." Unfortunately, the process does not work this way and it is not similar to the debt resolution process. The IRS is the U.S. Government. It has rules. It is a bureaucracy and similar to the military, you must follow the steps and meet the qualifications of the program or your Offer In Compromise will be rejected. The professional's role is to assist you in meeting the requirements from the standpoint of budget analysis and planning – but, believe me, there is no magic dust or special people to call at IRS to get the "best deal."

The basic premise of the OIC - is that you take the net value of your assets, inclusive of retirement and you add a component of your future income to arrive at the amount you must offer in order for the government to accept. So you can see – if you have significant funds in your retirement account or in equity in your home (something that is rare these days) the OIC is not going to work for you. Unfortunately, as a result of the phony advertising by the tax relief industry, few people are aware of this.

The new changes, however, are important if you have lingering tax debt and you do not have significant retirement or others assets. In that case, you should see if you qualify for this program. Under the old and new rules, your available excess monthly income is determined and this amount is used to determine how much you must pay to settle the tax debt. The amount is determined by taking your net income and subtracting the Standard Allowances for household expenses. These allowances are the same Standard Allowances discussed in Chapter 7 on Bankruptcy. Under the old rules, once the available excess monthly income amount was determined, it was multiplied by 48 and that became the minimum amount, plus the net value of your assets (equity in home, retirement and what is referred to as "dissipated assets") that had to be paid within 5 months of the date the Offer in Compromise was accepted. Under the new rules, the number of months for the multiplier has been reduced from 48 to 12. This means that the OIC under the new rules can be ¼ of the amount required under the old analysis. This is good news! Additionally, you can elect to pay over 23 months rather than within 5 months, but then the multiplier is 24, rather than 12.

The rules also have more favorable rules on what must be included as a "Dissipated Asset." Dissipated Assets are those assets that a taxpayer has transferred or used in the period prior to making the offer. In certain circumstances, the IRS can make you include those assets in the minimum amount of the OIC before it will be accepted.

Can I get an Installment Payment Plan?

You can always make an arrangement to pay the tax. The question is, "What is the best arrangement you can make?" The answer is – "it depends." For starters, in many cases, if the taxpayer's net income after the Standard Allowances indicates there is no money available to pay the tax, it is possible to get the IRS to give the file "CNC" status – which means "Currently Not Collectable." In this circumstance, the IRS will not require any payments on the old tax, but they will certainly grab any tax refunds that you have coming on returns as they are filed. (Hint – make sure you are not over withholding on your current tax year!). CNC status may be reviewed by IRS at any time, but generally, it is only reviewed every 2 years.

If you owe less than $25,000 in income taxes, under current IRS guidelines, you can automatically qualify for an installment payment plan to pay the tax over a 72 month period. If you owe more than $25,000 but less than $50,000 in income taxes, you can qualify for a 72 month installment plan but you are required to pay via direct debit. Under both plans, you can (and should) include a request that no lien be filed. Under the plans, you are required to stay current on your current tax obligations. The requirement of staying current on your taxes is an important and often overlooked item in planning. Sometimes, if you know you have a liability outstanding and a new liability on the horizon, it is a better strategy to file the return with the new liability and then set up the plan to cover the old and the new. This way, you start clean on the following tax year and decrease the chance of defaulting.

Payroll tax debt gives rise to personal liability for trust fund taxes. The trust fund is the portion of payroll taxes withheld from the employee's paycheck but does not include the employer's matching contribution for payroll taxes. The liability for federal payroll tax trust fund liability is nondischargeable in bankruptcy and if you find yourself in this situation you need assistance to address the taxes via installment payment arrangements and possible Offers in Compromise.

Again, keep in mind that even if setting up an installment plan, you are well advised to work with a professional who is in the business of addressing tax collection issues. Always refer back to the Golden Rule – do not represent yourself before the IRS.

10

Applying the Tools of Financial Crisis Management

Let me share with you how I analyze a person's financial situation to determine which tools of Financial Crisis Management should be employed to a particular situation. It is a step process of analysis.

Is Your House Way Underwater?

Since the house is typically the largest asset and liability a person has, the analysis begins here. Since 40% of homeowners nationwide are underwater, we need to assess whether you are underwater and by how much. For this reason, we need to identify the following information:

- What is the Fair Market Value ("FMV") today of your house?

- What is the amount of the first mortgage?

- What is the amount of the second and any junior mortgages?

- Are both husband and wife obligated on the mortgage notes?

- How far behind, if at all, are you on the mortgage payments?

With this information, you need to make a decision as to whether it is a smart play to keep the house or not? An important point here is whether the FMV of the house is less than the first mortgage. If the FMV of the home is less that the first mortgage then it is possible in a Chapter 13 case to "lien strip" the second mortgage and convert it to an unsecured claim (i.e. the same as a credit card bill). The best way to determine the FMV of your home is to contact a local broker in your community that you recognize from signs in the neighborhood so you know they are moving or listing. As part of the listing process or as a courtesy, the broker will do a market value analysis of the home. You want to know what the broker thinks it will sell for in today's market. Keep in mind, the amount you paid for the house in 2005 or 1995, the improvements you made to the home or the Taxable Assessed Value of the home are not indicative of FMV. If you can't (or won't) contact a broker, you can refer to sites such as www.zillow.com or www.eppraisal.com which provide market analysis of the home and area, but the range of estimated values tends to be quite significant in narrowing in on FMV.

Analyze Income and Debts

We need to make an assessment of your income and debt situation in order to determine if you are potentially eligible to file a Chapter 7 or Chapter 13 Bankruptcy. Is your income seasonal or regular? Are you self-employed or a wage earner? Are you drawing social security? These income factors are important because the amount of income is germane to whether you pass the Means Test under bankruptcy laws. If income is too high, eligibility for a Chapter 7 can be precluded and while you may be eligible for a Chapter 13, the amount that you would have to pay back to your unsecured creditors over the life of the plan may render the option too expensive compared to other alternatives such as Debt Resolution.

Social security income is important, as well, because it is not attachable by creditors (other than the IRS). Sometimes, with elderly people who are living exclusively on social security, the best outcome is not to file any bankruptcy or do any form of debt resolution as long as the right precautions are employed to prohibit a creditor from attaching assets if a judgment is obtained through the court process.

On the debt side, we need to carefully determine how much credit card and other debt you have, inclusive of any personal guarantees you have given. Whether the underlying nature of the debt is personal or business is also important because, as discussed earlier, there is a general exception to the means testing rules that permit a Chapter 7 case to be filed if the majority of the person's debt is business debt compared to consumer debt. A mortgage on rental property is a business debt, but the first mortgage on your home is a consumer debt. A second mortgage on your home, the proceeds of which were *used in your business* would normally be a business debt.

In one case, we represented a professional who had made the fatal mistake of financing his brother in laws printing business with personal guarantees of the bank credit line, equipment leases and substantial business credit card debt. On a personal level, he had a home way underwater with a first mortgage of $750,000 and second mortgage of $125,000, along with a boat load of credit card debt. His annual income was $300,000. Chapter 7 was an ideal solution to discharge all of the credit card debt and business liabilities, but he was eligible only if his business debt exceeded the consumer debt. With his large home mortgage, his personal debt was far in excess of the business debt. So what did we do? In this case, we let the house go to foreclosure. The lender in this case, submitted a full credit bid at the foreclosure on the home, which meant that he no longer had any debt on the mortgage note and no deficiency exposure. (We were actually surprised by the full credit bid). After the foreclosure, his consumer/personal debt still exceeded the business debt by $60,000. Our solution was to settle the second mortgage note on the foreclosed home. We called the lender and settled it for $10,000. We then waited for the bankruptcy preference period to run (90 days), filed the Chapter 7 bankruptcy and discharged all of the debt, preserving for our client his $300,000 income for future savings rather than paying off the debts of the past. Sure, in this case, we had to pay $10,000 to settle that second mortgage, but the result was far better than paying substantially more over a five year Chapter 13 of Chapter 11 plan.

An assessment of nondischargeable debts (those you cannot discharge even if you qualify for a Chapter 7 Bankruptcy) is also necessary. Non dischargeable debts include income taxes (unless you meet the discharge rules previously discussed) divorce obligations and payroll tax liabilities. Student loans, except in the most egregious case of hardship are also nondischargeable.

Decisions to Make

With the data gathered, the key decision that typically needs to be made revolves around the house. If the house is underwater but only by the amount of the second mortgage and a critical goal is to retain the home, then a Chapter 13 filing is likely the best approach because you can lien strip the second mortgage, giving it the same status as an unsecured credit card debt. If, however, your income is too substantial so that the cost of the program over 60 months is too excessive then an alternate plan is in order.

If house retention is something potentially desired, but not mandatory, then you have many more options. If you qualify for a Chapter 7 Bankruptcy, you should consider first pursing a loan modification of the mortgage so that you can lower your monthly payment on the home. By doing this, you create the opportunity to stay in the home as long as you wish by making the lower payment and since you've discharged the debt, once you decide you want to leave the home, you can just tender the keys or allow the foreclosure process to unfold without making payments and then vacate. An added benefit is that with the National Mortgage Settlement that was finalized in April, 2012 (go to www.nationalmortgagesettlement.com for details), the five major lenders, Bank of America, J.P. Morgan Chase, Wells Fargo, GMAC/Ally, and Citi are all responsible to provide some principal reduction on mortgages as part of the settlement. Because of this, in the current market setting, the chance of principal reduction in a loan modification is far better than it was in 2009 – 2011. Though there are no known parameters as to who is eligible, my take on the program is that the eligible person most likely must be in a position that his mortgage payment, inclusive of principal, interest, taxes, insurance and condominium dues (if applicable) will decrease under the HAMP 31% formula. The prospect that principal reduction may be available says to me "why not take a shot" at a loan modification – if principal reduction is included then keeping the home may make good long term sense. Either way, if you eliminate your monetary obligation on the mortgage note under Chapter 7 –then you have the best of both worlds.

If keeping the house is not an option and bankruptcy is not available to you, the best strategy in many markets is to short sell the home. A short sale, when successful, allows the exit from a house underwater without exposure on the deficiency that can arise from foreclosure and without tax consequences (provided you meet one of the exemptions from tax previously discussed).

Because a short sale entails falling behind on your payments (in order to gain the leverage needed for an approval and to influence the lender that it should waive the deficiency) your credit score is going to take a hit. As such, you should consider Debt Resolution of your existing credit card debt as part of the same process. Remember – the goal is to preserve future income for you and your family. Dumping the credit card as part of this process makes perfect sense. In this connection, careful planning is needed on the tax issue. Cancelation of credit card debt results in the issuance of a 1099-C. Your available exemption from tax on the credit card debt is only the insolvency rule since there is no bankruptcy and no real estate.

Timing is important. The underwater house often creates the necessary insolvency to avoid tax consequences on the canceled credit card debt. The order of events therefore becomes critical. If you short sale the home after you have settled the credit card debt, the underwater house constitutes debt to keep you insolvent after the credit card debt is canceled and to avoid income. You can then short sale the home and even if that creates solvency, you can rely on the principal residence exemption rule to avoid taxation on the canceled deficiency. If, however, you short sale the home first, you will not have the necessary insolvency when the credit card debt is canceled and the result will then be to create taxable income – so plan carefully!

Making the Right Choice

Several options present when attempting to find the correct strategy. Critical to your selection is keeping in mind the goal – "preserve future income for you and your family." A woman came to my office one day, having heard me either on the radio or at a seminar. She told me that she wanted me to resolve her credit card debt. She was certain this was what she wanted to do. She had $50,000 of credit card debt and was no longer able to pay the minimum payments. Her net income was around $36,000 per year; she had an IRA and no other assets. Her intention was to use the money from the IRA to assist in resolving the credit card debt. I explained to her – that debt resolution was an option – but not the optimal solution to her problem. Why? The answer was the cost. For her to settle her credit card debt, the cost would run around $25,000 over two years (inclusive of attorney fees @ 7.5% of the debt of $3,750) and the money would be coming from her IRA which is an exempt asset under the bankruptcy laws. Instead, at her income level, she easily qualified for a Chapter 7 Bankruptcy and the cost to her in legal fees was $1,500. So, I said, if the goal is preserving future income for you and your family, would you rather spend $25,000 over the next two years to *dump the credit card debt* or would you prefer to do it for $1,500? The answer was obvious, so I walked her down and introduced her to our bankruptcy section and we filed the case two days later.

Had this woman called one of the Debt Settlement companies there is no doubt in my mind that she would have been drawn into the slick marketing skills of these companies and would have signed up for their program – which charges 15% - 18% of the debt, settles for 50% or more on the debt, charges monthly fees and does nothing *to preserve her future income!* The point here is intended to illustrate the need for a comprehensive analysis as to the *best solution to the issues.* The difficulty is that there are few sources that will analyze bankruptcy, Debt Resolution, short sale, loan modification, foreclosure strategies and tax consequences together in order to glean the best path. Proper financial crisis management demands that such a review take place. You therefore must be sure that the professionals you employ adopt such an approach. If you can't find one who has such an approach, you will need to converse with the various professionals you are able to locate and then decipher the best strategy by applying the principles in this book.

11

Going forward with a Plan for Our Friends

We have identified the application of the Tools of Financial Crisis Management to Mike and Rita's situation - but what about our friends, Rich and Fairway, Jeff and Wendy, and Barry and Linda? Let's now look at their situation and decide the optimal course for them to pursue given the particulars of their situation.

Rich and Fairway – Now What?

Rich and Fairway are in a difficult position. The company is profitable but the Bank has called the company's loan and has delivered the word - get a new bank! The problem is – the credit market for small business remains extremely tight and the same criteria that caused the bank to refuse to extend further credit to Rich and Fairway exists with many lenders. So – what can Rich and Fairway do?

Rich has some options. The fact that his business is profitable means that he must immediately start shopping for other finance opportunities. An alternate bank or a private lender is the first option.

In this scenario – since the bank is the moving force, I have found that it is often possible to negotiate a short payoff (i.e. a substantial discount) of the business loan with the bank as an inducement to a quick and litigation free transition. This is the *one opportunity* for Rich and Fairway in this situation. There are no rules of thumb or indications of what can be achieved in this situation. The strategy is one of "feel your way" with the bank to try and gain that opportunity. At the same time, I believe it is prudent to come on strong against the bank, in writing and verbally, emphasizing the bank's unreasonable and unfair dealings so that, while exhibiting some level of diplomacy, the bank realizes that you are not going to make it easy if they elect to pursue their legal remedies.

While Rich is looking for an alternate lender or private investor to take out the bank, the next step in the process is for him to negotiate a forbearance agreement with the lender that will provide him a period to continue operating while he is looking for an alternate source. Banks will typically agree to a three to six month forbearance agreement in this situation and extensions to the term of the forbearance are common. Nevertheless, keep in mind that at the time you enter into the forbearance agreement you do not have any form of assurance that an extension will be granted.

The forbearance agreement itself has drawbacks. In virtually every instance the bank will include comprehensive provisions acknowledging the validity of the debt, waiving defenses and the right to a trial by jury. These provisions are typically non-negotiable with the bank and serve to bolster the bank's position if it elects to pursue its remedies to shut you down upon expiration of the forbearance period or if you commit a breach of the forbearance agreement's terms. The question immediately arises – should I agree to these terms for only a short 3 month forbearance term or should I fight now? This is a proper and good question. The answer is – it depends. In my experience, keeping the business afloat as long as possible with the goal of finding another lender or gaining a longer period from the bank with cooperation usually dictates the conclusion that you must accede to the demands of the bank on these provisions. Later, if the bank exercises its rights and enforces the forbearance agreement – we typically assert wide ranging claims that the forbearance agreement was entered into in bad faith by the bank and that the challenged provisions are not binding. These "claims" are just that – they are "claims" we employ as a means of further stalling and challenging the bank. In the end, a judge will typically rule in favor of the bank in such matters on the basis that freedom of contract principles mitigate toward enforcement of the contractual provisions the parties adopt. Getting to the ruling point, however, takes time, incurs expense (unfortunately for you, as well as the bank) and allows further time for negotiation.

There are additional strategies that need to be employed in Rich and Fairway's situation. You should also analyze the consequences of what happens if the bank does force Fairway into liquidation. In this case, you need to assess whether the bank's loan will be satisfied in full through the liquidation process or whether there will be a deficiency. If there is a deficiency, in all likelihood Rich has given his personal guaranty to the bank as additional security, so the possibility of Rich being sued for the balance exists. You therefore need to look at Rich's financial position. Are his personal assets held in a way that the bank will be able to reach them or are they out of reach?

If Rich lives in a common law property state (the majority of states are common law), has equity in his home (something rare these days) and it is held jointly with his wife as tenants by the entirety (or the equivalent tenancy under your state law) then so long as his wife has not guaranteed the loan to the bank, the house or equity in the house cannot be liened or attached by the bank. If, however, Rich's wife also guaranteed the bank loan, then the house and all joint assets are within the bank's potential reach. This is an important future planning point as well. For the most part, a business person who has an existing banking relationship will have to guaranty to the bank the business obligations, but if the lender asks for the guaranty of both husband and wife, this concession should always be resisted and only agreed upon if no other source of lending is available. Even if you have to pay a higher interest rate, I believe you should pay it rather than agree to provide joint guarantees to the bank. Joint guarantees limit your flexibility to avoid payment when you are in a default position.

If Rich has money in an IRA or 401(k), those funds are protected from the bank. If he has other assets, those can be problematic and he should take steps to place them farther from the bank's reach. This situation triggers what is referred to as "fraudulent transfer and conveyance" issues and is beyond the scope of this work. If all goes according to plan, I will cover these issues shortly in a new book (stay tuned) that addresses such matters.

So Rich's situation is serious but not hopeless. He needs to fight, seek a discount and find a new source of lending. If there are no new sources, he needs to scrap and fight with the bank and prove during the forbearance period that Fairway remains a good risk and that the credit term should be extended. Indeed,

Rich has a difficult task – but he has no choice other than to fight – so he must fight hard and smart.

Jeff and Wendy – For Better or Worse?

Life takes unexpected turns. This is what happened to Jeff and Wendy. They thought they were sailing through life – living well and happy, secure in the thought that their credit was strong and had placed themselves in a position that their spending habits were within reason given their strong credit and steady income. Jeff and Wendy – as result of the Financial Crisis have encountered a reality check. They have no savings – and were living off their available credit and equity in their home – and now they find out *they have no available credit and have no equity in their home.* So what do they do now?

For starters, Jeff and Wendy have every right to be angry and frustrated. At the same time, they have not lost their business or their income – and compared to many, the hardship they are facing is not as difficult to bear as those who have sustained major losses in income. Truth be told – Jeff and Wendy were living well, but not living smart. With their income level, they should have been emphasizing the need to save and have cash in the bank, rather than living on available credit and allowing a substantial portion of their after tax earnings to be wasted on interest expense rather than creating savings for retirement.

Jeff and Wendy have too much income to be candidates for bankruptcy. Their debt is personal and not business – so there is no getting around the means testing issues which precludes a Chapter 7 discharge. Chapter 13 is feasible but there is no second mortgage to lien strip and the amount of income is too great such that the creditors would be paid back all of the debt over the life of the plan. You might ask yourself, why am I immediately giving the "bankruptcy analysis" if there are other possible solutions? Why am I suggesting that Jeff and Wendy consider bankruptcy when they have not lost their business or jobs? The answer goes back to the goal – *to preserve future income for you and your family.* With this as the goal, my first analysis is how do we "dump the debt" as quickly and at the least cost as possible? The answer is – if bankruptcy works as a tool – it is the fastest and cheapest solution. In this case, bankruptcy does not work – but the process of analysis for other cases should always include this analysis.

Since we've determined that bankruptcy is not the applicable tool of Financial Crisis Management for their situation, we must look to other solutions. In this case, the analysis is not difficult. The solution as to the credit card debt is to settle it via Debt Resolution. Jeff and Wendy have $120,000 of credit card debt. Assuming average interest on these cards is now at 22% - the interest burn rate per year is nearly $26,400. Worse yet, Jeff and Wendy are in a 35% tax bracket and the interest paid on the credit card debt is paid with after tax dollars. This means they have to earn $40,615 pre-tax to pay the interest. This is 13.5% of their $300,000 annual earnings!

Monthly, they have been paying $3,300 per month on the cards. Depending on the mix of the cards, Jeff is looking at settlement costs on the cards in the 20% to 50% range. Attorney fees, in my view, should not exceed 10% of the debt. Our office has been doing major Debt Resolution work for 3 years and charges a flat rate of 7.5%. Notice I said "attorney fees" and not "fees." As already noted, you should avoid the slick and unprofessional debt settlement outfits at all costs. They charge 15% - 18% percent of the debt, they settle too easy at 50% and if you are sued they will not defend you in court. Worse yet - they are not licensed professionals so you have limited options to pursue remedies for their misdeeds. With the $3,300 monthly payments Jeff has been making - he has $59,400 of available cash over the next 18 months. This amount is right on target to fund the settlement and fees (if they are within reason) needed to eliminate the entire $120,000 of debt.

Now - let's take a look at the house. Jeff and Wendy are $115,000 underwater. Jeff's income is too high to meet the HAMP modification criteria, which in my view means it is highly unlikely that they would be eligible for any chance at principal reduction on a modification. Though they could probably obtain a modification with a potentially lower interest rate, the best expectation I see here is a re-amortized 30 year loan at market rates. In my view, such a modification does not serve the goal of preserving future income. If the home is underwater - why pay $425,000 for it on a go forward basis when it is only worth $310,000? The better solution - is to short sale the home now.

Combining both strategies for Jeff and Wendy can have a dramatic impact on their lives. They are presently in debt by $235,000 (the credit card debt + the negative equity in the home). Once the house is successfully short sold and the credit card debt gone they will have dumped $235,000 of debt, and Jeff's 401(k) plan with the same $100,000 will not be affected.

There are important tax implications for Jeff and Wendy. The short sale of the home will not be taxable so long as it is completed by 12/31/12 or later if extended by Congress under the principal residence exception. Important, however, is shielding the cancelation of the credit card debt from tax consequences. If Jeff and Wendy short sell the home first - after the sale, they will no longer be insolvent because the $100,000 in the 401(k) plan less the credit card debt of $120,000 means they are only $20,000 insolvent (assuming no other assets or debts). If they settle the credit card debt, they will be solvent post settlement by $100,000 and the cancelation of the debt would be taxable because they would not fit within the insolvency exception. Now - change the order. If they settle the credit card debt first - the negative equity in the home leaves them still insolvent to the extent of $15,000 after the settlement - which means they will not have to pay any income tax on any of the canceled credit card debt. Now, when they short sell the home - they will avoid the tax under the principal residence exception. (Keep in mind here, I am assuming both the first and second mortgages went to the purchase or improvement of the home). Timing is everything - as is the need to understand the principals of Financial Crisis Management!

To some - the Financial Crisis will leave scars and a bitter taste for many years. I don't see that for Jeff and Wendy. At the end of the day, the Financial Crisis for them will be an awakening and a blessing. The mistake of living to large off of credit happened to them. Like many, they were sucked into a whirlwind and could not get off. Lucky for Jeff - they were tossed from the whirlwind that day in the restaurant. On a go forward basis, the $40,615 in pre-tax income that was wasted on servicing credit card debt is now available to go direct to their retirement savings. As an added benefit, they are both out from a house underwater. The cost - nothing more than a short term hit to their credit score.

My clients like Jeff and Wendy have their own saying, "Thank you Amazon Express and BxA for your disloyalty."

Barry and Linda –
How to Get Back to the Good Life

Sad as it is, there is nothing I can say or do to give Barry back his business or eliminate the bad turn of events they have faced. But Barry and Linda have to move on and need to do so in the smartest way.

The business is gone - only the debt remains. Linda is obviously a talented real estate agent so her ability to return to income rests with reworking her real estate expertise to coincide with the short sale real estate market which is seeing solid activity as of mid 2012. Since the business was lost and they have no income, Barry and Linda clearly should file a Chapter 7 bankruptcy and discharge all of their debt that they can. This includes the Main Street Bank debt, any personally guaranteed business debt and the credit card debt. The payroll tax liability, however, is not dischargeable. In this case, neither is the income tax liability since it has not been three years since the due date of the return.

In addressing the $280,000 payroll tax liability and $70,000 income tax liability, Barry and Linda need help. Under the new rules announced by the Internal Revenue Service on May 21, 2012, Barry and Linda may be ideal candidates for an Offer in Compromise. I am assuming Linda is back to work and earning small commissions at this time and Barry is not yet earning income. If that is the case, assuming they have no other assets, an offer based on one year of current income (which is low at this point) may be accepted. Barry and Linda would need to raise this money in order to fund the settlement. I'm thinking in terms of a loan from family or friends. The key point here is to make the offer when things are at the lowest point because the result will be the greatest discount and least cost. If an offer doesn't work because of other assets owned by them or if their income has rebounded too quickly - the best interim option is for Barry and Linda to set up an installment payment arrangement. Since this liability well exceeds $50,000 there are no automatic programs which apply. The outcome of the installment arrangement will be dependent upon the ability of their tax collection defense attorney to persuade the collection officer that a reasonable payment is realistic from the perspective of their ability to pay and the government's interest to collect. If their income is low enough, they may be eligible for CNC (Currently Not Collectable) status which is presently revisited by IRS every two years.

Large lingering tax liabilities can be challenging *but are not impossible.* In Barry and Linda's case, the majority of this debt is personal only to Barry since he was the person assessed as the responsible party for the failure to the company's payroll taxes. This factor bids into the strategy of addressing the liability. In this case, it makes good sense to work first toward satisfying the income tax liability since both Barry and Linda are liable. With that covered; all future business ventures that Barry and Linda wish to pursue can be owned by Linda (as a corporation or limited liability company) rather than Barry until he is out from under the IRS debt. If Barry is working for Linda's new company - that's okay and in order to negate inferences that may arise that it is really Barry's company, I would adhere to sound (but not expensive) corporate formalities by making sure the corporate minutes are in proper order and make sure that Barry has a written employment agreement with the new company at a modest salary.

As you should see, there is no absolute simple guaranteed perfect solution for the tax liability. An Offer in Compromise might work and if so that would be great. If not, greater work will be required to keep things under control to preserve Barry and Linda's future income for them and their family. Their situation is difficult – but manageable.

12

Conclusion

The Financial Crisis has certainly taken its toll on us. The classic *American Dream of Home Ownership* was abruptly reversed to a nightmare with events that unfolded in rapid fire. The *Lehman Brothers* bankruptcy, the virtual collapse of the entire U.S. Auto industry and the explosion of the real estate bubble all came upon us in a three to four month span. Credit evaporated, property values tanked (and in most states are still declining) and unemployment skyrocketed.

With adversity comes opportunity and lessons learned. The lessons are clear:

- You can rely on a bank to provide you capital and money when things are good – not when they are bad.

- It is a mistake to feel secure based on your available credit and credit score.

- There is no better security than having Cash in the Bank.

- The Old Rules no longer apply.

- Preserving future income for you and your family is your responsibility – these are your shareholders.

- If it happened in 1933 and 2008, it can and will happen again.

The Opportunity – well I hope I've made it clear and provided you a direction. There has never been greater opportunity in our system to *Dump Your Debt*. So plan your course of action now and preserve your future income for you and your family. Good luck!

Websites to Visit

There are a number of websites that are helpful when it comes to investigating issues relating to Financial Crisis Management. The most important thing is that you need to be sure you are making decisions based upon current (and accurate) information. The Web is great – in its wealth of available information – but you need to be sure you are obtaining information that was not made up by a creative blogger or that is not outdated.

Let's start with websites that I cherish closest to my heart:

www.financialcrisistalkcenter.com – this is our home site for *The Financial Crisis Talk Center ("FCTC")* – our radio show airs on Saturday mornings. If you'd like to listen to the show, check the website for current station times and streaming information. Please feel free to call in and tell me what you think of *DUMP YOUR DEBT*. Podcasts of the radio show are also located on the FCTC site, as well as videos of TV appearances. The News section is a great place to check for breaking news relating to financial crisis issues.

www.facebook.com/FCTalkCenter - this is The Financial Crisis Talk Center's Fan Page on Facebook. Please visit the Page, hit "Like," post your comments and questions on the site and join in on blogging issues relating to the Financial Crisis, banks and government.

www.dump-your-debt.com – this site is dedicated to *DUMP YOUR DEBT* – updates to the content of the book and breaking news in financial crisis matters can be found here and at the FCTC site. In *beta* testing as of the release of this book is *The Financial Crisis Analyzer*. This is a web based program I have created that will allow you to input your relevant data and will yield an analysis as to which Tools of Financial Crisis Management are most likely right for you. The *Analyzer* will be free and part of the FCTC site, but updates on its progress and a link will be included on www.dump-your-debt.com.

www.thavgross.com – this is my law firm's website, THAV
GROSS PC – formed in 1982, the firm specializes in meeting
the needs of individuals and businesses and serves the
Michigan market. The site is divided between Business
Solutions and Financial Crisis Solutions and includes a News
section and topical information.

Here are sites that I find useful in addressing Financial Crisis
Management issues:

www.zillow.com – Zillow is a good site for estimating the
current value of residential homes. You simply input your
address and click and you are provided a wide range of
information on the property, recent sales and listings in the area
along with Zillow's Zestimate© as to Market Value and Rental
Value.

www.eppraisal.com – Eppraisal is another site that provides an
estimated value and also includes the Zillow value and a link to
Zillow. Eppraisal does not provide the level of detail that
Zillow does, but it is another source of relevant data.

www.housingwire.com – Housingwire is a useful site that
provides coverage of the U.S. housing economy. The site is a
good place to go for coverage of breaking housing news.

www.bretwhissel.net/amortization/amortize.html - this is my
favorite site to run amortization calculations. It's great because
any one of the fields can be held open to calculate the missing
link.

www.makinghomeaffordable.gov - this is the official
government site for Making Home Affordable. The site has
useful information and you can rely on it as accurate.

www.fanniemae.com - this is Fannie Mae's official site. Information relating to Fannie Mae owned or guaranteed mortgages can be found here.

www.fanniemae.com/loanlookup - does Fannie Mae own your mortgage? Go here to find out.

www.freddiemac.com - this is Freddie Mac's official site. Information relating to Freddie Mac owned or guaranteed mortgages can be found here.

https://ww3.freddiemac.com/corporate - does Freddie Mac own your mortgage? Go here to find out.

www.nationalmortgagesettlement.com -this is the official site that provides the latest and most accurate information about the National Mortgage Settlement that was reached between the 49 state attorneys general and the federal government with the five largest loan servicers – Ally/GMC, Bank of America, Citi, JP Morgan Chase and Wells Fargo. The site includes access to the consent judgments entered in the court proceedings, News relating to administration of the settlement, a Help section and Frequently Asked Question section.

http://portal.hud.gov/hudportal/HUD?src=/topics/avoiding_foreclosure - this is the HUD.gov site (U.S. Department of Housing and Urban Development). The sites most useful feature is that it acts as a major resource to link to other sites that provide assistance and information.

www.consumerfinance.gov - this is the official site of the Consumer Financial Protection Bureau. The bureau was established under the Dodd-Frank Wall Street Reform and Consumer Protection Act of 2010. This is the site to go to in addressing credit and debit card abuses and issues.

Acknowledgments

Many people have assisted me in this work. My most special thanks goes to Charles Thav, my partner of 31 years at THAV GROSS PC, our law firm, in Bingham Farms, Michigan. Chuck is my senior by ten years and was my mentor as an attorney, but more importantly, a terrific friend and example for me of how one should endorse life and family.

To David Einstandig, my co-host on *The Financial Crisis Talk Center* – thanks for having that unique ability to make me smile and laugh amidst the day to day trauma and stress of our law practice. Not to mention the back- up, support and superb skills you employ every day.

Special thanks also goes to Brian Small and Jenny Lingl who are regulars on the show, have provided technical assistance on many aspects of this work and with me have created what we believe to be a novel and new legal discipline. Thanks also to David Bennett, and all of the great lawyers, administration and support staff members of THAV GROSS PC, who have endorsed, adopted and given life to the concept of *Financial Crisis Management.*

Index

Become a Member -
The Financial Crisis Talk Center

- Weekly Radio Show – Saturday Mornings
- Website has streaming information
- Obtain latest news in Financial Crisis Issues
- Dump Your Debt updates
- Become a blog Member on Dump-Your-Debt.com
- Watch for the Financial Crisis Analyzer - Coming Soon
  Go to – www.financialcrisistalkcenter.com/join-fctc

Follow Ken Gross .. on Facebook
Financial Crisis Legal & Talk Center

Like

Go to - www.facebook.com/FCTalkCenter

Made in the USA
Middletown, DE
22 May 2019